THE WORLD IS ROUND

LOUISE MACK

Introduced by Nancy Phelan

ETT IMPRINT
Exile Bay

This edition published by ETT Imprint, Exile Bay 2021

First published as an Imprint Classic in 1993

First electronic edition ETT Imprint 2021

Texts copyright © ETT Imprint 1996

ETT IMPRINT
PO Box R1906
Royal Exchange NSW 1225
Australia

ISBN 978-1-922473-54-7 (paper)
ISBN 978-1-922473-55-4 (ebook)

Design by Hanna Gotlieb

INTRODUCTION

The World is Round was Louise Mack's first novel. It was published in 1896, a few months before her twenty-sixth birthday but the idea had been in her mind for some time. She often described how it had come to her one day in the train, suddenly and completely, 'ready-made from my brain', even to the title; but at the time she was absorbed in poetry and had postponed writing the book.

The incident is typical of Louise. Though she had a narrative gift and wrote many novels, she was primarily a poet and short-story writer who 'saw things complete'; slow methodical construction was not her way. What is not typical is that she delayed the writing, giving herself time to think and possibly rewrite. If, later on, circumstances had not led her into dashing off books in a hurry she might have left more good work.

Louise was the seventh child and the first girl in a family of thirteen. She was born in 1870, in Hobart, where her father, the Rev. Hans Mack was a Methodist minister. The Methodist church moved its parsons about on circuit and most of the Mack children were born in different parts of Australia. The family was always hard up, but for Hans and his wife Jemima the things of the mind came first and all their children were given the best possible education.

Louise, always known as Louie, grew up in a series of large, shabby, untidy parsonages; 'with no luxuries but plenty of books. Jemima, an obsessive reader, taught her children to read as soon as they were old enough; books, as necessary as bread, were constantly discussed and it is not surprising that Louise began to write very early.

All five Mack sisters were educated at Sydney Girls High School. While she was a pupil, no doubt inspired by eagerness to get into print, Louise started the school magazine, which still exists. She acted as editor, wrote stories and poems and when short of contributions, most of the other contents. At the High School she met Ethel Turner, who shared her ambition to write and who was for some years her closest friend and confidante: a friendship which was later affected by *The World is Round.*

The Macks, though poor, were hospitable. Their house was always full of young people and it was there that Ethel met her future husband, Herbert Curlewis, one of Sidney Mack's friends from the Law School. It was also to the Macks' house that Ethel and Herbert brought John Creed, another law student, an Irishman whom Louise later married.

Though the girls were both extremely pretty they were quite unalike in character and temperament. Ethel was reliable, well-organised, conventional, practical and self-disciplined, while Louise was erratic, intuitive, impulsive, unconventional, full of Irish charm and unpredictability. She could never resist a good story even if it made mischief, or a *mot juste* even if it caused hurt feelings. She was romantic, idealistic, an impractical dreamer but apart from occasional coolnesses the girls were inseparable, united in their longing for literary recognition and by their parallel love affairs.

Ethel realised her ambition in 1894 with the success of *Seven Little Australians.* The previous year Louise and her poetry had been 'discovered' by J.F. Archibald, the editor of the *Bulletin.* He made her his protegee and she became the pet of A.G. Stephens, the formidable *Bulletin* critic. Her work was published and praised, sometimes overpraised. She was taken onto the staff of the *Bulletin;* everything became easy, she was in demand. It was thrilling and wonderful but it was the old story of a young promising writer given too much attention and praised far too early.

By the time *The World is Round* was published, Ethel and Louise had married their young barristers. Both were still writing. In the next few years, besides working on the *Bulletin,* Louise produced two more books -*Teens,* the first novel published by Angus & Robertson, and its sequel *Girls Together.* Both books were semi-autobiographical, in particular *Teens,* which is set in Sydney Girls High School. But though the books were very successful, Louie's marriage was not. After four years she left her husband and set out for London, determined to make her name there as a writer.

Despite her disappointing marriage and her life as a journalist she was still romantic, impractical, full of ideals about literature. In order to write she lived in direst poverty in an attic in Bloomsbury and was literally starving by the time she finished her book, *An Australian Girl in London.* It was accepted by T. Fisher Unwin but in the meantime Louise was forced to take a job writing serials for the Harmsworth Press. It was work she despised; she called it 'lower literature', but it kept her alive and she did not intend to go on with it after her book came out. In her innocence she thought publication would make her fortune.

It did, in a way. *An Australian Girl* was enthusiastically received and given rave reviews. She became a Name; she also became the protegee of the great W.T. Stead, editor of the *Review of Reviews*, who praised her work and introduced her to literary London. But though *An Australian Girl* was a critical success it made little money, and to pay for her new way of life Louise had to go on with serial writing. To her surprise, and at first to her shame, she found she was good at it - once she had learnt the formula and how to write with her tongue in her cheek. But success was a dangerous gift. It brought in a great deal of money but for her 'real' writing it was the worst thing that could have happened. She had never had money before and had no idea how to manage it. She was like a child; there was not a saving bone in her body. Everything she earned was spent as fast as it came, on French dresses, furs, entertainment, travel; but as she guiltily churned out her serials to pay for her luxuries she consoled herself with the thought that one day she would give it up and go back to real writing words that are probably said today by countless successful television writers.

For several years Louise enjoyed a dazzling life in London.

Then she suddenly left it all and went to Italy, the country she always felt was her spiritual home. She settled in Florence, where she lived for six years, editing a paper, *The Italian Gazette,* and writing a novel, *Children of the Sun.* Like *The World is Round,* it is based on her own youth in Sydney and in some ways is her most appealing book.

There is a mysterious blank in Louie's Italian life. For two years she seems to have disappeared, then suddenly she was back in London, writing serials again, and also romantic novels. Working under pressure, sometimes on several books at once, she had no time to think or rewrite. The writing was careless, the plots and characters sometimes preposterous but the novels were enormously popular. Silly but harmless, they hurt no one but Louise herself.

When war broke out in 1914 she went to Lord Northcliff and persuaded him to send her to Belgium as a war correspondent. Her account of the bombardment and occupation of Antwerp, her experiences behind the German lines, disguised as a Flemish maid, and her final escape into Holland were later described in her book, *A Woman's Experiences in the Great War,* published by Fisher Unwin.

After the war Louise travelled all over Australia, New Zealand and the Pacific Islands, writing and lecturing. She had a happy second marriage to a man twenty years younger than herself and after he died she battled on, writing and publishing two more novels. Though surrounded by affectionate brothers and sisters, her last years were difficult; but she never became bitter, never lost her courage or her resilience and gusto for life. A true bohemian to the end, she died in 1935, aged sixty-four, leaving nothing, not even copies of her own books. She had never cared about possessions, regarding them as an obstacle to freedom, while money was purely for spending. She had always rejected security and despised caution. What she had valued and wanted was experience of life, and this she had had to the full.

In 1895, when T. Fisher Unwin wrote, enthusiastically, to tell Louise they would publish *The World is Round* they enclosed their reader's report. It described the book as 'a brilliant little study ... sparkling and witty and told in a graphic style'. After nearly a hundred years it still seems sparkling and witty. It is a slight, unpretentious novel but it succeeds because the author did not try to exceed her capabilities. Louie's talent was lyrical; weighty, ponderous subjects were anathema to her. Though her touch was light it was not brittle, her satire was sharp but not bitter. She had perception and feeling but the book is not sentimental, though there are moments of genuine pathos, and these were the days when strong men wept (in novels) and women wore 'great breast-knots of violets' on their womanly bosoms.

The story skims a long, a mused, insouciant, at times mischievous. There is none of the laboured archness that often passed for humour in young new writers and old bad ones of the period. The main characters are well-drawn, the minor ones skilfully evoked. Louie's 'graphic style' is natural, pointed, economical. This economy makes the book seem curiously modern. The chief betraying signs of a period-piece are the conventions-Musgrave's outrage when Harrison refers to Jean by her christian name; the masculine comments on women; the dialogue of the lovers. Did people really say, 'I love you, my own boy' ... 'My saint, my saint!' ... 'Oh, my small sweet lovely child'? Apparently they did, for similar speeches crop up in contemporary novels; besides, when Louise was writing this book she was up to her eyes in a love affair with John Creed and presumably knew what she was talking about.

The then current male attitude to women's brains and female writers was certainly not the author's. 'I believe your talents as a literary woman to be feminine in the extreme and of the very smallest account,' says Musgrave, crushing Jean's hopes. 'I thought that [spite] was a woman's motive,' says Harrison; and as Musgrave leaves an evening with Jean's admired but fatuous friends he thinks that 'No surer proof of the femininity of Jean's intellect could have been found than that gathering of people.'

Louise was not a feminist in the way that her sister Amy was, but she never saw women as inferior. She knew from her remarkable mother's example that they could be as strong, resourceful and intellectual as men, and she certainly never considered herself a lesser writer because she was female. In her own experience she had not encountered discrimination from editors because of her sex. She liked men and was extremely popular with them, but for all her romantic ideas she had no illusions about the games that women were expected to play. On page 40 she says '... men don't like women to be clever enough to see through them but they like a woman with brains enough to appreciate their appreciation' and on page 58, 'A woman is flattered when a man tells her about himself and other men; a man is bored when a woman tells him about herself and other women.'

The book has many funny, true, clever, if mocking touches: the would-be writer trying to write; inane party conversations; the bereaved heroine sitting on an uncomfortable stool because she feels it more appropriate to grief than a comfortable chair; the man who 'knew a great many quotations but could not often get a chance to bring them aptly into his converse.' Her wit, aimed unerringly, is sometimes so subtle it almost escapes notice. She is merciless with pretentiousness but has sympathy for human predicaments, though she also sees their humour: poor hapless Harrison taking out his handkerchief to wipe the girl's tears and finding it covered with ink; the evening party when there was not enough coffee. She writes lyrically of the beauty and mystery of the Australian countryside, about Sydney Harbour, the Gardens at night, and scathingly about Australian girls who 'ape the English accent; say "gude-bai" and "hoa d'you du".' And from time to time there are glimpses of a deeper, questioning Louise behind the clever *degagee* satirist.

Much of what she wrote is in some way autobiographical. *The World is Round, Teens, Girls Together, An Australian Girl, Children of the Sun* and *Teens Triumphant* all draw, to a certain extent, on her own early years. In *The World is Round* a number of settings and incidents are taken straight from life: 'the great bare schoolroom in Elizabeth Street, whose walls had been convicts' work' ... the nervous art teacher's stumbling speech to the girls . . . the shabby drawing-room that is a photographic reproduction of the Mack drawing-room the children eating bread and dripping out in the kitchen the moonlight picnic on the harbour.

These transfers are harmless, but she did not stop with them.

Like all novelists she based her characters on aspects of people she knew, but she did not always bother to disguise them. The originals often recognised themselves, sometimes with amusement, more often with anger. She had sometimes done this and got away with it in her short stories, but *The World is Round* was widely read and to make matters worse a newspaper review reproved her for ridiculing well-known and easily recognisable people. The reviewer even identified one of Louie's targets, a woman she considered a poseur . To readers in London these characters and their fatuous conversations would have been merely amusing, but cultural Sydney and its fringe dwellers did not like being laughed at.

The fuss had barely died down when a rumour about the book began to circulate. It was said to be an attack on Ethel Turner, that Louise had written it out of spite and envy for Ethel's success. No one knew if the rumour was true but people could see that the heroine, Jean, was, like Ethel, a pretty fairhaired girl with literary ambitions; like Ethel she has a Latin motto-*Nulla dies sine linea* ('in sepia on rough paper')-over her desk to spur her on; she runs a children's page and dashes off little pot-boilers for the newspapers. Like Ethel, she is loved by a barrister but is reluctant to marry; she says things that Ethel had often said to Louise, but unlike Ethel she has no talent at all and wins fame through a trick.

Though Louise denied the charge, at first glance she seems guilty; but is it not possible that when she 'saw' her story it came to her devoid of personal implications, that she registered only its impact and shape? Later on, as she worked on the novel, needing details to build her characters, she undoubtedly helped herself to bits of Ethel's, and Herbert's lives, perhaps reassuring herself that the book was fiction, that no one would take it as true, for Ethel had shown she had talent. It was thoughtless, reckless, dangerous, but was it deliberate malice?

Louise was distraught, while Ethel dismissed the rumour with contempt; but Herbert believed it and forbade Ethel to see Louise again. She refused, but the friendship was damaged, things were never the same again and slowly the women drifted apart. After Louise left for London there were very few letters and though in later life they sometimes met, they had little to say to each other. Their temperaments were too different, their lives had grown too far apart.

This incident helped to perpetuate the myth that Louise and Ethel were rivals. They were rivals at school when they both ran magazines, but as adult writers their work was completely different. Ethel's forte was writing for and about children; Louise wanted to write for grown-ups, about life, love, passion, sin, grief and so on. One has only to read a page of *The World is Round* and one of *Seven Little Australians* to see that even in their first books the work of these two writers was totally unalike.

What happened to the thoughtful, perceptive writer hinted at in *The World is Round?* It has often been said that Louise did not fulfil her early promise because she was praised too soon, told she was good and encouraged to rush into print when what she needed was time to think and develop, as well as to be disappointed. She wrote instinctively; writing to her was a natural function, but without proper guidance and criticism her work too often became facile. Facility, with a fertile imagination and love of inventing stories, made her a successful romantic novelist but it eroded her talent, and years of formula writing elbowed aside the poet. She never lost her poetic awareness but had little occasion to use it. Haste, lack of reflection, putting words on paper before they were ready robbed them of their true value; it was quicker and easier to write of trivial events than try to express deep, difficult thoughts and emotions.

Yet in all Louise's books there are glimpses of the writer she might have been. Even in her most idiotic novels there are occasional patches of true feeling or sensitive descriptions, reminders that she could have done better; a source of exasperation but also of regret.

Would she have left more good work if she had not written romantic novels? if she had not had to write for a living? if her life had been different, if she had had a husband to keep her and give her the time her writing needed? Or was her own nature, her restlessness, her passion for travel and thirst for experience the enemy of her talent? She loved writing but even more she loved living.

NANCY PHELAN, Sydney 1993

1

Musgrave

Sydney was revelling in the clear, cold weather of June, the most delicious month of the Australian seasons.

There was a fire in James Musgrave's chambers, and three men sat smoking there one luncheon hour. They were Alec Harrison, a teacher of painting, also an artist; Musgrave himself, and young Montagu Burnes. They had all been reading a story from a paper which Montagu held in his hand, and they were now going to discuss it. Monty had asked them to do so.

'She will never be anything great,' said Harrison.

He looked sorry for the truth of the statement as he made it. 'She is cut and dried for nothing more than a children's journalist. No nerve, no freshness, no insight.'

He threw the paper on the floor. The 'she' referred to was Jean Burnes, his sister. Musgrave picked it up. He let the others talk on for a minute or two.

'Humour is the gods' dripping,' he said then. 'It will spread many a slice of dry bread. This last story of Miss Burnes' now! Gushing, adjectival, girly-girly, artificial, full of strange evidences of the feminine mind, with wrong constructions and wonderful meanings given to ordinary common-a-garden words, reminiscent, over-run with false sentiment, yes-yes, it may be all that, as you both have said. Yet two little strokes of humour in this story have betrayed a curious fact to me. I shall watch with interest for its further development.'

'What fact?' 'She has genius.'

'Who? Jean? What rot!' said Montagu. 'Rubbish!' and Harrison shook his head.

'Very well,' said Musgrave. 'It may be rot, and it may be rubbish. It's genius all the same.'

'Oh, Mr Musgrave!'

A new voice broke in upon them, a clear voice with sweet tones in it, but no briskness, and with a slight colonial accent. The door, which had been but half closed, was pushed open, and a girl walked in, a girl with grey eyes, and babyish contour.

'I heard! I couldn't help hearing! You are talking of me!

I heard my name. I heard you say' -she gasped in her excitement, and made a little choking noise, 'that-I-lam a genius.'

The three men sprang to their feet. Harrison flushed violently. Montagu put on a firm look as one who told himself, 'What I means I says, what I says I sticks to.' Musgrave looked calm, but more annoyed than any of them.

'It was unpardonable of us to criticise you,' he began. He threw away his cigar. 'We had no--'

'I don't mind. Not at all. I forgive you freely, oh, ever so freely! You, Mr Harrison, I forgive you, and you too, Monty.' She nodded her head at both of them, and smiled with a smile which she tried in vain to check. She did not want to look *too* pleased, to look idiotically delighted, but how was she to help it. It is not every day that one hears oneself called a genius by a genius. And Musgrave was a genius.

She turned to him.

'I thank you from the bottom of my heart,' she said, half with the air of saying more than she meant, yet evidently meaning it thoroughly. Her face grew serious. The archness disappeared, 'I am so glad you think so. I daresay that you would never have told me if I hadn't forced your hand, as it were. Fancy she finding out what you really do think of me! Oh, I am so glad. You're a little bit clever, you know, yourself. I didn't tell you so before, but I don't mind telling you now. I'll try, and try ever so hard, now that I have heard you say that, I feel sure there is power in me to do great things.'

'I am sure there is,' said Harrison. 'I never doubted it. What I meant was-'

'Rubbish,' she said. She half closed her eyes at him, then burst out laughing.

'Oh I forgive you,' she said. 'I forgive you. Don't look so frightened. To tell the honest truth, I don't care a bit what you think of me. I don't think you're at all a good judge. Do you, Mr Musgrave? Now, do you think the man who could paint a lake and some waterlilies on a lookingglass could be a good judge of anything?'

'But you asked me to paint it,' said Harrison.

'Well, but that was no reason for your doing it. And you did it so well too. Disgracefully well. Especially the cow. There was a cow, too, you remember. You have done them before—dozens of them. How could you be a judge of-'

'I never did such a thing in my life before,' interrupted Harrison hotly.

Then she laughed.

'Really? No, I know you didn't. I'm sorry. I didn't mean it.'

'And I don't follow the logic of your result.'

'Oh well, I'll explain some other time. I am in such a hurry now. Aunt is waiting at the bottom of the stairs for me. I only came in to tell you, Monty, to call for me at the Vincents' at ten o'clock, unless you will come earlier and spend the evening.'

'On nothing. No, I'll call at ten. Don't keep me waiting, though.'

She shook hands with the other two men, and to Musgrave she said: 'Will you come and have dinner with us tomorrow night? Do. I want you to tell me what makes you think so highly of me, and to tell me some more nice things about myself. I want to talk to you now. You have become suddenly interesting.' She smiled, said good-bye, and hurried away.

She had scarcely gone before Montagu jumped up hastily, said, 'I forgot to tell her-' and rushed after her. The other two were alone together.

'Miss Burnes gave you rather a drumming, my child, didn't she?' said Musgrave.

'"M?' said Harrison. He had noticed that his bootlace had come undone, and he stooped his head to tie it.

'Are you as much in love with her as ever?' Harrison did not answer.

'I was in love with her myself once.'

'You were?'

'Yes, but she laughed at me from morning till night. She kept me near her, yet she seemed to push me away. She half made me her friend, yet she snubbed me, teased me, and was perfectly candid with me always. I suppose I was bewitched with her. She is pretty, you know,' an assertion that made Harrison stare by its calm audacity. 'And then somebody told her something about me, and when she spoke of it to me and I denied it, she did not believe me. Told me coolly that she was very sorry, but she did not believe me, and would not pretend to believe me, which meant, in effect, that she considered me a cad. She likes me nevertheless, I know she likes me.'

'And was what she heard true?'

'True,' said Musgrave. *'True?'* He got up, and walked to the window. There was nothing to see out there but the roofs of buildings, yet he gave those considerable attention for a minute. 'What is "true"' he said. 'Is there really such a thing; as we conceive of it? I am not going into detail with you, Harrison, but if it was true it was false, and if it was false it was true. As a matter of fact, it *was* false, therefore it was also true.'

"The lie that is half a truth?" said Harrison. He knew a great many quotations, but could not often get a chance to bring them aptly into his converse. He felt rather proud of this one; tried to look unconscious, and was aware that he was making a dismal failure of it, even though Musgrave was not looking.

'Yes,' said Musgrave. 'Something like that.'

'Did you get cut up about it?'

'Cut up? I didn't like it. Of course. Who would? But I don't mind now. I have squared myself with the little lady. You needn't tell young Monty this-he is a fool, and wouldn't understand-but you will, I daresay. If you don't you'll pretend to. I saw her coming up the street while you were finishing her story. I knew she was coming here. As we were talking of her, I heard her footsteps on the stairs. I raised my voice purposely, I noticed that the door was not quite closed. When I called her a genius I knew she was pausing just outside. I meant her to hear me. And she did. I pretended to look annoyed.'

Harrison stared at him.

'That strikes me as a jolly low thing of you to do,' he said at last.

'Does it?' said Musgrave. He was perfectly certain of the hold he had on Harrison. In an insolent way he was aware that when he had once made a man like him, no power on earth, save his own, could take that liking from him. The gods had given him the greatest, most fearful, most inexplicable of all the gifts a man can have-fascination. They had detracted no whit from it, either, by endowing him with a full consciousness of his attraction. What might have made another man conceited, made him insolent, careless, but more attractive than ever.

'Didn't you mean what you said about genius?'

'Mean it? Great Scott! Why, she has as much literary ability as that poker-and not as much originality. It never pokes the fire twice in the same way.'

'The fire is always changing...'

'Exactly. But her matter never changes. It is always the same-and her style too. She will never do anything, never, never, never. But she will never, never, never believe it-now.' 'Why did you say that, then?'

'Oh, I knew it would please, and yet be bad for her. I suppose I was conscious that it was the very worst turn I could have done her. I am only half sure, though, that those are my reasons. It is only in books that a man knows exactly why he says a thing-that he has one reason, and one only. In life one never does a thing for less than a hundred reasons, and one can't always put a finger on the fundamental one. Ah, Monty, did you catch your sister?'

Harrison looked at his watch. 'I have a class at two,' he said. He rose. And now, at the mention of the word 'class', you saw that though his hair was curly, and his eyes young and bright-looking, there was a little hole on the left side of one boot, and the elbows of his coat-sleeves were shinier than his linen. He put his hat on, and looked about for a roll of drawing-copies.

'Harrison,' said Musgrave, 'by the way, I think my motive was what they call spite.' He smiled sadly into his pipe. 'I thought that was a woman's motive,' said Harrison. This was his idea of being crushing. He went towards the door.

'Good-bye, old chap,' he had said to Montagu. 'Good morning, Musgrave,' was his farewell to the other.

This was his idea of being cool. Then he went away.

2

Harrison

There were between twenty or thirty girls waiting for him. They sat at desks in a great bare schoolroom, in Elizabeth Street, whose walls had been convicts' work, with their blocks and pencils, and drawing boards, and squares of bread, neatly arranged before them. There was no teacher in the room at that minute, and they were all talking together in loud whispers, interspersed with giggling. They lowered their voices when Harrison came in. Some of them whispered back 'good day', in return to his general greeting. But the minute he turned his head to lay his hat upon the shelf, their talk was as brisk as ever. He walked to the table, and struck the gong there. Once, twice, three times ... The voices died down, died down. 'Silence,' he said. They sank away altogether, buzz and hum disappeared, there was dead silence in the room.

He stood before the table, and tore a bit of paper to shreds with nervous fingers. Then he cleared his throat, and made a little gesture of picking at his chin.

'Before you begin-er-your work to-day,' his eyes downcast, his fingers still fumbling, 'I want to-er-say a few words to you about-er-Art. Some of you here are-er-very eager, and-er-very young. You would like to begin and finish a new-er-subject every time, take it home ready to-er-frame. Your-er-great ambition is to-er-see how many pictures you can-er-hang on your drawing-room walls before you finish-er-with me. You would perhaps like me-er-to give you cows and water-lilies to paint on looking glasses. I will never do it. Last week the-er-subject I gave you was a very-er-interesting one. The study of a boy's head, I left it to your own discretion whether the head was to beer-a beautiful one, or an-er-intellectual one, or a study of an uncommon type. All I asked was that you studied your subject, and remembered the lessons I have been giving you lately on the-er-head. Now look for a minute at your results.'

He opened a portfolio on the table, and proceeded to hold up, one by one, his pupils' attempts at the subject in question.

The first head provoked a seething giggle.

It was a boy with the left ear lower than the right; the right eye rounder than the left. The nostrils were mere slits. The neck had apparently been dislocated, and the head was still in an impossible attitude. It was so grotesque as to be absolutely painful.

Harrison pointed out its defects. His face was very grave.

James Musgrave would have laughed to excess at a scene like this. Harrison felt a stirring at his soul that killed laughter and brought lines out across his forehead. This was no joking matter to him, this class meant bread and butter. There was no knowing what might happen to him if their work continued as bad as this was. He would probably be sent away.

'Don't laugh, please,' he said simply, taking out the next sketch. 'This is work, not play. Be earnest about it.'

He held up the second sketch. A perfect roar of laughter greeted it. The girls stared and laughed, and stared and laughed. Harrison, standing holding the sketch up before them, cried 'Silence,' again and again in vain. They were beside themselves with amusement. At last, in the midst of the uproar, the door opened, and the head of the school walked in. She bowed to Harrison, and went across the room to where he stood before the table. The girls stopped laughing in a trice.

'Can you not keep better order than this, Mr Harrison?' she said in an undertone. 'These girls are disturbing the other classes so much that it is impossible to go on with their work. Why are they laughing so uproariously?'

Harrison turned the canvas toward her. 'I was commenting on their home work,' he began, but before he could get any farther a strange smile lit up the Principal's face: her mouth widened against her will.

'Oh, Mr Harrison,' she said. 'What-how *very* funny. She too began to laugh.

'What is it? said Harrison. He could see nothing laughable about this abominable school-girl sketch.

'It is a caricature,' she said.

'Yes. An unintentional one.'

'Oh, surely not. The likeness is speaking.'

'What likeness?' He stared at the pictured face that was staring back into his. 'Who is it a likeness of?'

'Why of you,' said the lady. 'Surely you knew it.'

Harrison turned very white. 'It is meant for a likeness of me, is it?' he said slowly. A strange light came into his eye. His mouth twitched. He laid the sketch on the table and looked at it in silence. He himself was rather a handsome fellow, though his shabby and old-fashioned clothes did their best to hide it. He was young, twenty-five at the most, with a thin face, a broad figure, slightly stooped from the shoulders, brown wavy hair, and faithful, dog-like eyes, clear, brown, humble, and patently the mirrors of a true soul, if an unsophisticated one.

Before him lay the study of a man with an elongated head, long, narrow, flapping ears, a small child mouth, and great, sad, round eyes. Yet it was unmistakably Harrison.

The Principal stopped laughing. She pulled her face together.

The enormity of the thing dawned on her. She saw Harrison standing white and set, looking with the caricature of himself before him, and the girls all sitting watching with pricked ears and curious eyes. She turned to them suddenly.

'Girls,' she said in a ringing voice, 'who did that?' She pointed authoritatively towards the sketch.

She was answered at once.

'Me,' said a little girl in the back seat. She was the smallest girl in the class, and was sitting at the end of her desk with her hands folded neatly in her lap, and her eyes looking straight before her. She was the youngest girl in the school, a tiny creature with a little wisp-like pig-tail of flaxen hair, and a great white pinafore whose embroidery ruffles reached almost to her small sharp chin. Also she was Star Burnes, Jean's younger sister!

'What?' said the Principal. 'Stand up whoever spoke.'

'I did,' said the little girl.

She stood up at once. She was very calm, and had a gentle look in her eyes.

'You,' said the Principal. 'You!' Her voice rang with anger.

'And may I ask why you did it?'

'For fun,' in a deprecating voice. The Principal turned to Harrison.

'Mr Harrison,' she said, 'On my own behalf, I must apologise to you for the impertinence you have been subjected to in my school to-day. Star Burnes has been guilty of the grossest rudeness and impudence to you. I can scarcely think of punishment severe enough for her. Expulsion ... ' She looked very grim.

'No, no,' said Harrison, quickly. 'It doesn't matter. Don't punish her. I don't want anybody punished for my sake. I'm a scapegoat myself.' This bitterness was a little unusual, but Star was Jean's sister, and was the one girl in the class who represented a life to him. The others were only pupils.

He put the drawings into the portfolio, and began to tie it up, as though to change—and end—the subject. The Principal told Star to bring her board, and come and sit in the front desk under Mr Harrison's eye. She put aside her day-reckoning for a while. A few minutes after she was called out of the room.

Harrison turned to the black-board. He had drawn it forward to within two feet of the front desk, and he stood in the intervening space, just' in front of Star. His back was towards the class. He was showing them something on the board. A small end of his handkerchief was sticking out of his coat pocket, his old-fashioned Paget coat. There was a row of ink-bottles fixed in all along the front desk.

Very gently Star stretched her hand forth, and drew his handkerchief from its place. A little more, a little more, till she had dipped the half of it into an inkwell. Harrison worked away earnestly, explaining gravely all the while.

Presently he smudged some chalk on his nose. He drew his handkerchief out to wipe it away. In a moment he was inked from brow to chin.

'What.' He felt the dampness on his chin. He put his hand up, and rubbed. It was black, and wet. He looked at his handkerchief. Ink all over it! He stood transfixed.

'Who did this?' he said. He hardly knew how near he was to bursting into tears.

'I did,' said Star, rubbing her bread-crumbs vigorously.

'You?' said Harrison. Then his eyes blazed, and his lips trembled. He looked at her for a minute, then made a step towards her. Then he paused ... She was Jean's little sister ... He must not touch her ... He was the drawing master ...

'I will never forgive you as long as I live,' he said. He went straight out of the school.

In the playground he stopped at one of the taps, and washed his face with another handkerchief. Then he went out of the gate. He told himself that he would never go back.

He walked on a long way without seeing anyone. People passed in dozens, for it was now nearly five o'clock, and office life was pouring itself into the streets. But he saw none of them. He found himself walking fiercely along Hyde Park, under the cool shadows of the heavy Moreton Bay fig-trees, before he knew just where he was going. His brain was in a whirl. He could see again and again the grinning class, and the little fairhaired devil who had made mock of him. Where, in all the length and breadth of the land, was there a man so tried, so cursed, set in such ignominy, yet bitten through and through with such ambition!

Good God! what was the use of his living? He would not live. He would live no longer. There was something wrong with him, some crook in his composition. He had noticed it often. It was a horrible thing, a cruel, stinging, unaccountable thing. Something about him, he knew not what, invited ridicule. Oh, how often he had noticed it! Perhaps they thought he did not see - James Musgrave who laughed at his theories, and called him my child in a patronising way; Monty, who was ruder to him than to any man he knew; all the men about town who had a sort of 'here's a joke' look when they talked to him. They all made game of him. Because he said nothing, they thought he did not see.

What was there to laugh at in him? He tried to see himself.

He could see himself only as a man always in deadly earnest, crushed by poverty; baffled and beaten at every turn, fu ll of longings, uplifted sometimes with a sense of deathless power, cast down at other times into the lowest depths of depression, and despondency, but always trying to do his best.

Was that ridiculous?

Was it his face, his figure that amused them? His speech?

His theories? His clothes? Involuntarily he shut his eyes, squeezed them up tight.

'My God, what a cad I must be getting to imagine such a thing as that.'

In his simplicity he killed that thought before his mind had time to revolve around it. It came upon him with a rush that he was young and yet a man; a man with a heart and a soul, and a mind all agrope for food, but starved, cramped, repressed, all the world afar from him. His people were in Scotland. He had come to the Colonies alone seven years before. His mother believed he was doing well. She herself was so poor that she wrote occasionally to him for money. He had no influence and had sold just one picture in all these seven years. He earned about £3 a month by teaching. Was such a life worth living? And then there was Jean. It was only in accordance with all these things that he should have come to love Jean. His love was perhaps the most hopeless, futile love in all the world. In his boldest moments he could never imagine himself more blessed than to have her hand for a space and to kiss it. When he thought of her now a mist came over his eyes, and he breathed a sigh that was almost a groan.

'I've got that snake-poison,' he said. 'It won't show. My mother will never know.'

'Mr Harrison! Mr Harrison!' cried a little voice behind him.

He turned round, and stopped.

There stood Star, hatless, white-pinafored, dishevelled, with locks of curl less flaxen hair blowing over her eyes and forehead. She had evidently been running for a while. Her face was very red, and her eyes were full of tears, and, as he looked, these tears brimmed over, and splashed down slowly over her nose, and cheeks, and chin.

'I ran the other way first-down Elizabeth Street. Oh, do speak to me again! Do speak to me!' Her voice changed to a wail, and she clung to his hand and sobbed, looking piteously up into his face all the while. 'You must, you must!' She made a little excited movement with her foot, beating it again and again upon the pavement.

'Dearie,' said Harrison, tenderly, a broad Scotch accent coming out suddenly in his speech, 'don't cry, don't cry. Oh, please, please, don't cry.'

He put his hand in his pocket, and drew out his handkerchief to wipe away those terrible tears of hers. What evil fate gave him the inky one? He doubled it up in an agony of fear lest she should notice it, and thrust it back into his pocket. He remembered he had wet the other, and left it on the school-tap to dry.

'Star,' he said, agitatedly, 'Star, Star.'

But the tears still fell. They seemed to cut a sharp and edgy way into the tender places of his soul. He could endure them no longer. In desperation he stooped down, and taking hold of the edge of her pinafore, he lifted it to her face and rubbed her eyes and cheeks on the hard insertion trimming.

She put her arm up limply, and let it fall round his neck. He bent down a little.

Then he had to kneel right down, she was pulling him so hard.

There they were, right in the middle of the asphalt path, with the street not ten feet away, and the Moreton Bays overhead, and people passing perpetually by them, the light-haired hatless little girl crying on the neck of the drawing master, while he knelt before her, and carefully and tenderly wiped away her tears.

It was characteristic of him that no sense of the strangeness of the situation stirred in him. The people might have been a thousand miles away. He thought of nothing but this little crying child.

'Oh de-ear,' she sobbed.

'Are you so very sorry?' whispered Harrison. 'Y -y-yes,' she sobbed. 'I c-can't help it.'

'Then let us be friends again, and forget all about to-day.' He made a movement as though he would have risen, but she held him closely, and her sobbing breaths went fluttering along his throat.

'I I-like you more than anyb-body,' she whispered brokenly, 'y-you're so nice.'

She drew his face round towards her, and kissed him with two little warm soft kisses that had all her heart in them.

It was seven years since ... He thought of his mother.

Perhaps that was why his eyes filled. 'God bless you,' he said.

Her hand ached afterwards from the strength of the pressure he laid upon it.

Then he got up, and picked up his hat, and patted her hair down, and took her back to the school. He waited outside while she got her hat and books, and then went with her till she was safely at her own home.

As he walked back towards his lodgings he had quite forgotten that there was such a thing as snake-poison.

The world, that is always searching, and learning, and questioning, and analysing, and finding out new things, has yet to discover the magic equal to a kiss.

3

Jean

Musgrave duly went to dinner with the Burnes as he had been bidden. He put on his dress-clothes, expended a little extra Pomade Hongroise on his moustache, liked the look of his face to-night in the glass, remembered that his mother-poor little soul-had thought him handsome in the days gone by; then went out, and forgot trivialities in the absorption of a rather unique situation.

In the Colonies, about one family out of a thousand dons dress garments for the evening meal. A few of the wealthy social leaders of Darling Point and thereabouts follow the example of Government House people, but the great majority of Sydney people sits down happily to its seven o'clock roast beef in its ordinary every-day garb. It denounces dressing for dinner as an affectation of the first water.

The Burnes were an exception. Old Mrs Mainwaring, the aunt, was what Colonials are wont to describe as a 'real old English lady'. In her case this meant an immense nose, a backbone like a poker, grey silk dresses, and a profound contempt for cheap Colonial society. Jean and Star had been on her hands since babyhood, but though she had endowed them with much of the erectness of her carriage, she had utterly failed to bend them to her theory that 'God made the Englishman; the turf the Colonial'. Jean, indeed, agreed that it was nicer to meet men who were not afraid of giving you a chair, or of waiting on you with a slightly exaggerated deference and gravity; who knew what to do with their hands, and really raised their hats from their heads when they bowed to you. But like all Australian girls, she declared Australian girls a great improvement on their English sisters. So long as they were satisfied to be Australian, and not to ape the 'English accent'; say 'gude-bai', and 'hoa d'you du', and affect unnatural and ridiculous modulations in their tones. She summed them up as being bolder, braver, more unconventional, and consequently more interesting; more ambitious, more independent, smarter, brighter, more natural, less graceful perhaps, but more passingly pretty than English girls. Star preferred Australians of both sexes. She frankly disliked politeness. She said it bothered her to say 'thank you' so often as one had to in the company of Englishmen. She preferred men who did not inquire after her health, or stand up when she came into the room. She was twelve, but had many matured opinions on men and morals, and *no* objections to broad vowels.

Musgrave took a Woollahra tram, and in half-an-hour he found himself alone in Mrs Mainwaring's drawing-room. A bright asbestos fire was glowing in the grate. The floor was polished to an extravagant sheen. The rugs were Russian bearskins and white wolf, there were rich and costly Chippendale chairs, old china, photographs, laden book-shelves, a faint odour of pot-pourri, great jars of arum lilies and slender spiky daffodils and jonquils-he could almost have imagined himself back in his mother's drawing-room at Kensington. A great 'possum skin thrown invitingly over a easy chair in the corner gave the one alien touch. He had grown used to the similarity between Australian homes and English ones; had got over his wonder in the past three years, at finding such refinements of taste as confronted him, even in far bush towns and stations, but to-night it struck him afresh, the quickness of this new land to follow every change in the mother-country's ways.

The door opened, and Jean came in.

'I am so glad to see you,' she said, meeting his hand with hers and giving him a straight glance from her eyes.

He thought how fair she looked, and how uncommonly grave. The lids of her eyes-surely they were a little reddened. Something subdued seemed bearing down her usual elasticity of glance and tone.

'How are you?' asked Musgrave.

'Mr Vivian is dead,' said Jean. She took her hand away and sat down on an uncomfortable little gilt milking-stool, with a dim idea that it was more suitable to her grief than the case of the comfortable wicker chairs. Her skirts fell round her on the floor, they were black and gauzy. In her bodice she had fastened a great breast-knot of violets. Two or three of them leaned over from her dress, and laid their sweet dark heads against the whiteness of her neck. A handful of them were pulled loosely through the satin of her belt. Musgrave did not understand that these were meant for mourning. He mistook them indeed for something festive and told himself that girls with golden hair looked adorable in black and violets.

'He died yesterday,' went on Jean, looking at the beading of her shoes, and twisting a leaf between her thumb and forefinger. 'It was very sudden, horribly sudden. I was there spending the evening you know, and he went upstairs to his study to write. When they called him for supper they found he was-' she shuddered - 'Mrs Vivian hasn't cried yet, and they say if she doesn't soon, her brain will turn.'

Looking up suddenly she caught Musgrave's eye. He was just then consumed with a vision of the same Mrs Vivian as he had seen her last, speaking on Local Option in the Domain, her bonnet awry, her nose very red, and all the strings of her tongue unbound. Would it take so very much to turn that brain of hers? For the life of him he could not help wondering. His mouth twitched.

'Oh!' he heard Jean say, in a horrified voice. Then-

'Oh, you *are* wicked. You're *laughing!* Actually *laughing!*

And I'm telling you about a man who is just dead.'

'No, no,' said Musgrave. 'It wasn't that. It wasn't really I-I-can't explain, but-'

'It doesn't matter,' said Jean. 'It doesn't matter in the least. All the same I think it horrid of you.'

'I assure you-'

'Oh, the world is a hard place,' said Jean, suddenly, apropos of nothing. She put her hand up, and drew it quickly across her brow, then stared hard into the fire, and Musgrave saw to his horror that her eyes were full of tears.

'Miss Jean,' he began. Then stopped, not knowing what to say to her.

'I am sorry,' he murmured, in a tone that was just loud enough to reach her ear. Suddenly she turned and looked at him.

'Isn't it terrible,' she said, her wet eyes looking straight into his, 'when you know you can do work and someone who knows you will persist in thinking that you can't.' She looked at him solemnly, and a cold shiver went down his back. Harrison had told her!

'Mr Vivian was like that about me,' she continued. Musgrave breathed again. 'He was very fond of me, you know, but he would always say to me, "I didn't like that last thing of yours, Jeanie."'

'There is always someone who "didn't like that thing" of one's.'

'He said, "If you hope too much for yourself you'll be disappointed. It is only a fit that will work itself out eventually." That used to make me so cross. Once I said, "Well, I manage to get myself accepted," and he said, "That means nothing, child, absolutely nothing. It's a bad sign that you should think it a good sign."

'He was what one might call a wet blanket.'

'But he always told me he discouraged me for my own good.'

'Did you ever know anyone who discouraged you for your bad?'

'Has anyone ever discouraged you?'

'Good-! Till I was thirty the only encouragement I ever had was the discouragement of the people whose opinions I valued. I considered there must be something in me if sensible people wanted to make improvements on me.'

'That's good,' said Jean, after a pause. 'You turn one round so easily. Are you supposed to be very logical?'

'The Bar has much to answer for,' he said, with a grave face. 'Mr Vivian had a mind,' said Jean. 'He was no ordinary man. He ought to have known.'

'But you are probably out of his range. I admit his mind - it was superb; yet greater minds have made false literary conclusions.'

'Dear old man,' said Jean. 'To think that he is dead, and I will never be able to show him what I can do.'

Musgrave had a sudden feeling of revulsion.

A pair of clapping hands the less-was that what her grief meant.

'And oh, poor Mrs Vivian.'

The sorrow in her voice put him to shame.

'I daresay you will find plenty more people who will need to be convinced,' he said consolingly.

'Oh, of course, I know that. But you think I can do it, don't you?'

'Yes.'

He was looking at her when he said it, too.

'I don't suppose I will ever be a George Eliot, or a Thackeray, but perhaps I may be a-'

'Miss Austen.'

'*Miss Austen!* oh, surely I'll be something b-I mean surely I won't be like *her.*'

'She did some good work.'

'At any rate I'll be somebody. I'll be myself. Oh, it is so good to know that you have such a high opinion of me. You have published three books, haven't you?'

'Yes, three.'

'They were great successes too. Oh, I've taken a new lease of life since I heard what you said of me to Monty and Mr Harrison. Repression may be good for some souls. It isn't good for me. What woman was that who, when somebody said to her "Repression has made you what you are," answered, *"But not what I might have been?"* I want encouragement, and praise, praise, praise. It is like wings to me. I can soar to the clouds on it. Not the praise of nobodies, but of people with brains, men like you, who find it easier to cavil than to see good points. In my mind's eye I have always a male audience. I only write for men. I really think few women are worth writing for, do you?'

'Good Heavens,' said Musgrave, under his breath. He pulled at his moustache, and stared hard into the fire. He was thinking of those poor little stories of hers.

'Don't think me conceited,' Jean said earnestly. 'I know how much I have to learn, and how hard I shall need to work. Last night I sat up for hours over my new story. I worked it up to a climax, but had to leave it there. I didn't know exactly what to do with it. Perhaps you could help me. It is this way...' She plunged into it straightway.

As she talked she turned her head away a little, and looked into the fire till her profile was towards him, and her fresh arch mouth showed him its sweet half-bow. It opened, and closed, and opened over her little sharp white teeth in a fascinating way.

Musgrave found himself watching her intently.

How adorably pretty she was, her face so chased with light and swift unlooked-for changes. Her eyebrows would be elevated suddenly, and her eyes would gleam and be merry, or her face would grow grave, and her eyes and mouth; and a wrinkle would run along her forehead, as the narrative took on a more serious hue.

He went into a dream, and everywhere, all through the wanderings of his thoughts, that piquant rounded face was before him.

'And then I don't know what to do. What would you do?' said Jean. He woke up suddenly.

There was Jean looking at him and waiting for an answer, and he had not listened to a word she had said to him.

For a moment he was stupefied. But only for a moment.

A brilliant Machiavellian inspiration seized him.

'What did you think of doing yourself?' he asked. But before he knew if she had discovered him, the door had opened, and Mrs Mainwaring came in. He was saved, and a moment later came dinner.

4

The People Who Came In

After dinner some people came in, and there was no more continued talk between Jean and Musgrave that night.

It was the fourth Friday of the month, and Mrs Mainwaring was At Home to such of her acquaintances as were welcomed at her house.

A fairly representative gathering of Sydney's upper ten filled the drawing-rooms. Musgrave looked round, and remembered Jean's remark at dinner, 'There are some rather clever people coming tonight.' He wondered where they were.

Finding that he could not talk to Jean, he amused himself by watching everybody, and talking to no one. He was in a mood of cynicism to-night, and his brain made rapid and scornful comments on what was going on around him.

Just behind him a young man with a high collar, a big nose, and a certain ruddiness of cheek that betrayed him as an English suckling, was talking to a young woman in daffodil satin. 'Did you see "Pagliacci"?' said he.

'Oh, yes!' she said, 'I saw it three times.'

'Bai Jove! I thought it was very good,' said he.

'Oh, I thought it was lovely,' said she. 'Didn't you?'

'Yes, I thought it was awfully naice.'

'Wasn't the end sad though? I thought it was so sad.'

'Yes, it was. It was *awfully* sad.'

'It was frightfully short, wasn't it? Didn't you think it was short?'

'Yes, I thought it was awfully short. It was *awfully* naice though, was it not?'

'Oh, it was *lovely.*'

Musgrave's enjoyment of this was something too intense to be described. If they would only go on! He picked up an album and began to look interestedly through it. The pair seemed to have exhausted themselves, though, for the moment. They were silent for such a long time that he was going to look about for some fresh food for scoffing when they began again.

It was the girl who pushed the ball this time. 'Have you ever read a book called *Lost in the Zodiac?*'

'No, never read it. Who's it bai?'

'I don't know. I never look who a book's by. Do you?'

'No. Tell you an awfully naice book. Read it on board coming out, *Miss Nobody of Nowhere.*'

'I haven't read that. Is it good?'

'Very good. Very er-er-interestin'.'

'Is it? I must get that. Do you know who it's by?'

'One of these French fellows, I think. Sounds like a Frenchman. One of these detective plots, you know.'

'Oh yes, I know. Like that book everybody was reading the other day, I forget the name of it.'

'Yes. Sort of detective yarn you know. Very good.'

'There's a book called *A Painted Polyanthus*'-Musgrave gave a sigh for a man he knew who would have revelled in this with joy as keen as his own. 'They say it's very good. I haven't read it yet.'

'Neither have I.'

Musgrave was disappointed. 'Have you read *Speech in Passing?*'

'Oh yes, I read that. Awfully naice, is it not?'

'I thought it was lovely. I *cried* over it.'

'No? Did you? Bai Jove!' leering sentimentally.

'Yes, I couldn't help it.'

'The "sulky man"- he was a rum cove, wasn't he. He *was* funny, wasn't he.'

'I don't think he was a sulky man at all.'

'Neither do I. They only called him that,' boldly. Her voice changed. "And Ida died," she quoted, in a tone that suggested to you that she was just going to burst into tears.

Musgrave turned his head to see how she was looking. Just as he thought. Her head was a little on one side, her eyes were staring sadly straight in front of her, and her mouth was doing its best to look pensive and full of feeling.

"And Ida died," she said again.

That was evidently the one point about the story that had struck her most impressively. Unfortunately hers was not the face to express the feeling she would fain have conveyed. Her nose was large, and boned to the tip. Her eyelids suggested a difficulty in meeting over her eyes; her mouth carried the same suggestion with regard to her teeth. Her hair was dressed exactly as nine out of every ten girls wore their hair just then, a bun at the back, covered smugly with a net, a curled fringe coming to a point on the forehead, and flattened also with an invisible net, as truly unbecoming a fashion as the giant goddess has yet set women imitating. Her father was a Supreme Court Judge who sat on the bench with stiff and conscious dignity, so she was generally described as aristocratic-looking. Musgrave, who did not know her as the Judge's daughter, called her ugly.

Jean came and carried the suckling away, and the Judge's daughter sat alone, waiting for a victim. Fate, in the shape of Jean, decreed it should be Musgrave. She came towards him. 'Let me introduce you to somebody,' she said. 'You're all alone.'

'Won't you talk to me?'

'I can't. I must look after people for a while. It's the duty of a hostess not to enjoy herself,' sweetly.

'Well - Miss Jean.'

'Yes?'

'Don't introduce me to that lady behind you. As you are strong, be merciful.'

'I will,' said Jean promptly, immediately pouncing on the Judge's daughter, and making Musgrave known to her with ceremonious formality.

'You can talk books together,' wickedly, 'Mr Musgrave loves reading,' to the girl; 'Miss Pomedda is the secretary of the Woman's Literary Society,' to Musgrave; who groaned inwardly, and gave her a reproachful glance, at which she smiled a little as she moved away.

'Are you fond of reading?' asked the Judge's daughter.

Musgrave had rapidly decided how to talk to her. To encourage her would be sinful.

'No,' he said. 'I'm a Philistine.'

'Fancy! Are you really? Don't you read at all?'

'The newspapers and the serial stories in the magazines and reviews of things. I find that quite enough, and the best way to improve your mind if you mix with literary people.'

'I always read the reviews of books,' she said affably. 'Then you know if a

31

book's good or bad.'

'Do you?' said Musgrave innocently. 'I didn't know that before. And are *you* fond of reading?'

'My two favourite pastimes are reading and thinking,' she said, with well-bred pensiveness.

'Good Lord,' said Musgrave under his breath. 'What did you say?'

'Who is that stout woman by the piano, with short, grey hair, and silver shoes?'

'Why, that's Mrs Raymonda. Don't you know her? She has just written a novel, and put my father and Lord Carrington into it. My father thinks very highly of it.'

'I wish somebody would write a novel, and put me in it,' said Musgrave reflectively. 'I am sure I should think highly of it-if I read it.'

'Shall I introduce you to her then?'

'Oh, thank you, don't trouble. What is this lady going to do?' They were clearing tables and chairs away from one end of the room, where a lady stood, assuming a slightly theatrical attitude.

'She is going to recite,' said the Judge's daughter, watching interestedly.

The reciter stood for a minute with her hands clasped loosely before her, her head a little bent, as if in acknowledgment of tumultuous applause from the silent and embarrassed audience.

Then she raised her head slowly, showed her teeth, lifted one hand, and began.

'The Patriot,' she announced. A moment's pause. Then - "It was roses, roses, all the way," she called in a loud voice, with a strong affected masculine flavour about it.

And then an awkward thing happened to her. She forgot what came next.

She stood there, pressing her under-lip hard with her forefinger, and gazing agonisedly at Jean, who was nearest to her, and vainly trying to beat up the forgotten lines from her treacherous brain. There was a dead pause. The people in the room, who had just carefully turned their eyes away from the painful spectacle of a drawing-room reciter's face, had now to look back again, to find the reason of this silence.

'This is too rich for anything,' said Musgrave in a jubilant voice to his companion. She did not hear him. Her lips were making violent gestures to somebody across the room. Though no sounds issued from them.

Nobody had the courage to speak the second line of the broken poem. Some of them must have known it, but nobody dared suggest the forgotten cue. Everybody felt as if the voice that suggested it would echo round the room for hours after.

At last, after what seemed an interminable time of horror, the reciter's hands fell clasped again before her, and in a slightly different tone from that of her last utterance, she began straightway to declaim Calverley's 'Shelter'.

She had gone from the ken of ungentle men,

Yet scarce did I mourn for that;

For I knew she was safe in her own home then,

And the danger past, would appear again.

'For' - impressively pausing a minute to allow their smiles to accumulate-'She was a water-rat.'

But everybody had been wrought to such a pitch over 'The Patriot' that they had not the spirit even to smile now. They knew they ought to, but they could not.

She sank into a chair, and smiled nervously at the carpet.

The murmured 'Thank you's' fell flatly on the air.

Musgrave turned to the Judge's daughter.

'Did you ever in your life see anything so ghastly. If that woman belonged to me I should take her home and shoot her. A woman who recites in her friends' drawing-rooms should certainly be put to death.'

She turned her head, and looked at him with eyes so horrified, astounded, and full of naive wonder that such a man should dare to exist, that he felt the colour rising to his cheek. 'That lady is my sister,' she gasped. Then she rose and crossed the room, and left him alone in stricken silence.

It was quite five minutes afterwards before he smiled again.

He sat and reflected on many things, and vowed fiercely to himself that he would never again spend the evening in such a way. It consoled him a little to see a man, for whose intelligence he had a profound respect, come in late, and settle into hopeless misery as he realised that all these people were here to talk, and to be talked to, and that he would probably be expected to add his quota to the rest of the entertaining. He was a man with a fine head, wild eyes, and one tooth out in front. A tall awkward-looking man, who kept his tongue tied up six days in the week, and on the seventh blossomed into as brilliant eccentric and interesting a talker as one could meet. He fell into the hands of the lady who had written the novel. She talked to him, probed him, laughed to him, argued, and did her best to make him appreciate her capabilities. She prided herself on the sympathy of her intellect, and whenever the man made a remark, she had a way of wrapping his remarks up in mental brown paper, which he loathed to unfold himself. She worried him to explain himself, and to tell her exactly what he meant, she smiling sweetly the while. As soon as he could, he worked his way to Musgrave, and looked piteously at him.

'What's the matter, old man?' asked Musgrave. He knew what the matter was all the same.

'I have never been here before,' said the other. 'Montagu asked me. Where is he? I don't see him.'

'He's somewhere about. What are you looking so down-in-the-mouth about?'

'Musgrave,' said the other impressively. 'There are a terrible lot of well-meaning people in the world.'

'There are,' said Musgrave. 'Terrible is the aptest adjective for them, too.'

'But the people who can understand a man are damned few. I'm going home. Are you coming?'

Musgrave persuaded him to stay till civility had had her meed of him. Then they crept away together, Musgrave whispering to Jean as he bade her goodnight, 'I will be revenged for that lady in daffodil.'

He thought it all over as he walked home to his lodgings in Macquarie Street, and he told himself that no surer proof of the exceeding femininity of Jean's intellect could have been found, than that gathering of people. One after the other they came before his mind, and he smiled contemptuously. He wondered how Jean could endure evenings of such unmitigated boredom, the company of such utterly uninteresting people. Tolerance was not Musgrave's strongest trait. He seldom bore with anything. He swept things out of his way if he did not like them. And his intolerance vented itself on nothing so bitterly as on shabby and pretentious intellects.

The consequence was that he had a larger score of enemies than any man about the town. His opinions were never veiled. He was always careless of giving offence, and many who appreciated and fully admired the immense brain powers of the man, hated him personally, especially when away from him. He took it all as a matter of course. Now and again when a man whom he had openly despised, and spoken of as of no importance, gave sudden and unexpected proof of his mental endowments, Musgrave would candidly acknowledge his surprise, would possibly tell the man himself he had not thought it was in him, and would end by gracefully and unobtrusively impressing his own magnetic individuality upon the other's unwilling consciousness. He felt that he could always do this when he chose to take the trouble, and he rested satisfied with the thought that those whom he liked, liked him. His indifference to those who did not like him was one of the most characteristic things about him.

He felt almost angry with Jean for knowing such people.

Why on earth did she cultivate them? He could hardly believe though that she regarded them as intellectual, and yet he remembered her remark, 'There are some rather clever people coming to-night.' Poor little Jean!

He walked on, and a moonlit mist hung over the silent gardens, and over the curving, silvery harbour that washed the feet of the gardens' long green slopes. The air was sweet with rich tropical flower-breaths; the great magnolias by the iron railing were whitened with heavy blossoms, and the pittosporum was all out in flower, the garden gates were locked now, but he turned in through the ever open gates close by, and entered the domain. Down a long walk shadowed thickly with the overhanging branches of great Moreton Bay fig-trees, and scattered underfoot with their round brown windblown fruit, over a stretch of untrimmed yellow grass, to the rise that looks out across the harbour where it curves into Woolloomooloo Bay, the seats beneath the trees were nearly all occupied, for this was the favourite sleeping place of Sydney's poor and destitute; but he found an empty bench near the wall of the ugly art gallery, and sat down there, and lit his pipe.

Away behind him in the distance the post office clock told out the hours with its placid chime; one o'clock, half-past, two, half-past two, three. He sat on smoking, thinking, dreaming.

The sense of exquisite solitude, begotten of night and trees and a sky with a few dim stars in it, swept over him strongly. The world with all its make-believes of pleasure, has little better to give than to be alone in a perfect stillness, with a great city close at hand, alone with the night and the stars, and the world as God made it, to hear the whole fall of a little leaf, from its dropping from the tree to its stealthy settling in the grass beneath, or the tiny trail of some insect along a withered branch, or the rhythm of a bough blown or bent by the wind; to feel the height of the sky above, and the breadth of the world around, and to come forth for a moment from the suit of mail in which daylight conventionality has sealed her children, to leave behind you, with one free leap, all thoughts that run in grooves, all stale time-worn truths, and to come, by no set route, in all that stillness upon a strange new wonderful being, yourself.

There is horror in it, but there is the divineness of wide open eyes.

This happens sometimes even to those who have travelled a lifetime and never looked on themselves. It happened this night to Musgrave, but it did not move him. He fell to thinking of his past. It did not read as a bad thing, but-he knew. He knew with an unswerving knowledge that he had lived for himself for fifteen years, and let neither God nor man stand in his way. Especially God.

But no intention of altering his course stirred in him now.

He meant to struggle just as hard as ever for what he wanted. It was Jean now. He meant to win her. 'She *shall* love me,' said he, 'I will *make* her. She shall marry me, and give up all these flabby people.' He considered himself calmly. He knew as well as anyone that there was a masterly strain in his intellect, a swift reliable insight that showed him in one flash things that other men took years to see, and he told himself that he had never tried for anything yet without getting it. He had struggled for success and won it. A brilliant career lay behind him, and fame and substance before him. He had never allowed himself to be turned aside from anything he wanted.

'I will make her love me,' he said again.

Jean in her own room that night, with her gold hair gleaming under her brush, was thinking of Musgrave.

She was always ready to acknowledge him as the cleverest man she knew. At the bottom of her heart she had a little proud feeling that so clever a man should care so much for her talk and her society. She had a friend who would tell her with rude candour that the men she knew would never help her build her brain, and Jean rejoiced to be able to bring Musgrave forward in defiance of this statement.

And yet, in spite of her admiration for his intellect, she was thinking now: 'But I can't like him. Really, I can't like him. I think his mother must have spoilt him when he was a baby. He's selfish, and contradictory, and inconsiderate, and horrid to people he doesn't like ... I know he was making fun of everybody this evening. I wonder what he thought of them. I don't think it's nice of him ... He was nice when we talked together before dinner. Sometimes I almost like him, but I don't think I could ever believe in him. I wonder if he really said to her, in so many words, "My God, I love you." That was what she told me he said. And the very night before he had professed to care for me. I believe I liked him then. Certainly it was rather horrid of Elsa to tell me, but she didn't know that he-I-. She felt she must tell somebody ... It is all very strange-' She followed up that train of thought to the end.

Then she turned her thought to his warm spontaneous praise of her work.

'If I had not overheard it,' she said. 'I could scarcely believe that he meant it all.'

As she sat there she looked up, and saw her face in the glass before her, with the gaslight shining full on her golden hair, and pure, soft skin. She forgot Musgrave. She put her elbows on the table and leaned her face in her hands, and looked solemnly at herself in the glass.

'Could anyone look like that and be clever? I don't see one sign of cleverness in my face. My eyes look silly, my nose has no character, my hair curls too low on my forehead, my chin is as round as a peach. Everything about my face is so round. I always had an idea that a clever face must be long. What a silly little face I have.'

She stared hard at it.

'After all,' she concluded, 'it is nice to be pretty as well as clever. Mr Musgrave would probably not like me as well if I had a drab complexion, and a hooked nose. Nor Mr Harrison, poor boy.'

She smothered up her thoughts, and went to bed. Her last thought ere she slept was a happy one.

'I must work hard now. There's a future before me, if I only get to it.'

She passed into sleep, planning to have the motto 'Nulla Dies Sine Linea,' in sepia on rough paper over her study table.

5

In Which The Friend Is Brutal

Jean sat upstairs in the little study that looked out across the harbour, writing or trying to write.

There were piles of foolscap on the table before her, and ink and many broad-nibbed pens, but the paper was most of it blank. Some sheets had half a line on them-scratched out generally. Some had only one word, also scratched out. Not even the broadness of the broad-nibbed pens was smooth enough to carry her thoughts along to-day.

'Down in the valley,' she wrote very slowly, 'grew a little vine.'

There she stopped, that she might read aloud what she had written.

'Yes,' she said to herself. She bit her pen-handle for a minute, changed little vine to Little Vine, then began again.

'Over there to westward lay a long, green valley, and from its grew up a Little Vine.'

She paused and looked at that for a while.

'From its what?' she said. 'What's the word? What do I mean? From its arms? its sides? heights? depths? Depths sounds best.'

She filled the blank with 'depths.' Then she read the sentence over again, once, twice, but before she could read it a third time, she scratched it out.

'Oh dear,' she said. Her sigh was suggestive of hard work, and attendant weariness. She dropped her pen, and stopped to pin her hair back from her cheek. She had to take a hairpin from the knot at the back of her head to do this, and the withdrawal of the hairpin brought the whole mass of her hair tumbling about her shoulders. The sun, shining in through the open window, caught it, and sparkled in it, and burnt it till there were red lights in it as well as golden ones.

'How pretty,' she said. 'I'm glad I've got nice hair.' She let the 'Little Vine' go out of her head, as she leaned it down on the table, and made her hair sweep over the papers in a patch of sunlight. She looked at it with half-closed eyes.

'Girls with red-brown hair are supposed to be wonderfully fascinating. I wonder if it means girls whose hair gets red in the sun. Perhaps I'm more fascinating when the sun shines on my hair. Perhaps I'd better be always in the sun when there are men about.' Her eyes were shut now, and her voice was dangerously suggestive of sleep.

'I'm coming in,' said a voice, some time after. A girl opened the door as she spoke, and came in. 'What are you doing?' she asked.

'Writing,' said Jean, sitting up suddenly, and blinking.

'On your hair? and with your eyes shut?'

'I was just looking at my hair for a minute, and my eyes must have shut themselves,' lamely.

'I believe that's how you spend most of your worktime,' said the friend, candidly. She took her hat off, and threw herself into a downy easy chair. She was taller than Jean, and much thinner, and had enjoyed the reputation of being the prettiest girl at the university, in her own year, or in any other. There was no good feature in her face, except her short and shapely nose, but the light in her eyes and the expressiveness of her mouth made her strangely attractive. Her eyebrows were two fine, black triangles, that moved up and down when she laughed and talked. Her teeth were very white, and very crooked, and her mouth showed them all suddenly when it smiled. Jean said it was those crooked teeth that made her so fascinating. The eyes were brown, with curly black lashes, and though they were not very large they mirrored every smile and frown that crossed her face. Sometimes they were absolutely bubbling with laugher, and sometimes, when they were looking at a man, they would be most soft and gentle, and other girls would say this girl was flirting.

She was slight and very graceful. Not even the extreme shabbiness of her attire could hide her grace.

'I've had the blues,' she said. 'Badly. That's why I came to see you. I can't write a word. I can see in and out of my brain, and it's empty as an eggshell when the egg's been eaten. It's horrible. I want to buy a new pair of boots next week, and I can't even write half-a-guinea's worth of verses.'

'Poor Kiddie,' said Jean, whose patent toe-caps shone beautifully.

'What about you? Are your ideas shrivelled too. Or does genius flow? I see you've got a new box of J's, and two new novels, and an empty teacup.'

'I'm writing chapter ten of my book,' said Jean.

'What book?'

'The one you were reading here the other day.'

'Oh, Jean, surely you're not going to keep on with that!'

'Why not?'

'I wouldn't.'

She looked Jean firmly in the face.

'I read the first five chapters, you know,' she said.

'Well?' said Jean.

'You have a kitchen fire-place.'

'Oh, but I've altered them since then. I've scratched out nearly all the adjectives, and altered all the girls' names, and the men's too. I call Dorothy, Mary; and Guy, James. And Estelle, and Gladys, and Antony I altered to Alice, and Rhoda, and Dick. Those were your chief objections.'

She watched the friend's face.

The friend sat up, and clasped her hands round her knees. 'It's a funny thing,' she said, looking straight in front of her. 'When you, or anybody who likes me, cuts me up, I let it pass over me like a west wind, nasty, but not harmful. I believe I have a kink in my composition. I believe in the praise of my enemies, but not the blame of my friends. There's an epigram for you. The meanness of my nature makes me suspect some personal undertone when my friends blame me. But there's none of it in my criticisms of you. I honestly believe there's none. I'm not jealous of you. I don't envy you. There's *none,*' still staring straight in front of her.

Then her eyes came to Jean's face, and she laughed.

'That will prepare you for what I'm going to say. You have two pairs of shoes at a time, and four pairs of gloves. You have unlimited tickets for the dress-circle, and an account at two book shops. You have admirers too, not to speak of lovers, and you send your MS to be type-written. You can bear it.'

'Go on,' said Jean. 'You're going to be brutal.'

'I'm going to be candid. I didn't come to be candid-or brutal. But I'm in the mood, so I'll tell you-I have more brains than you, Jean. That's the enunciation we're to go on. The authority is myself, and the fact that I never write when I've been reading novels, and drinking tea. And about that story of yours-'

'Go on. Go straight.'

'I will. You've no originality. You've no freshness. You've no wit. You have a certain amount of style, but it's borrowed, it's not characteristic. It's reminiscent. I hate your stories. Why do you always give your girls golden fluffy hair, and sweet ripe, scarlet lips? And no brains. I'd make them as bald as the woman before she used Barry's Tricopherus, and as white about the lips as if they had eaten a barrel-load of starch, but when they spoke I would make them say something smart, and to the point, something worth saying, and worth listening to, not a string of empty meaningless frippery.'

She stopped suddenly, and looked blankly at Jean.

'I wonder why I don't do it,' she said. And the naiveness of this filled the study with peals of laughter for many minutes after.

Then Jean began to defend herself. She was not likely to let so sharp an attack go unrepulsed.

'You must remember,' said she, 'that I was only twenty-one last birthday, while you are twenty-four nearly. You are about the only girl I really know, so how can I make my girls talk cleverly? I copy nature. How can I make them epigrammatic?'

'How can you make them pretty?' digging a ditch.

'Oh, but you are pretty,' falling in at once.

'Jean, dear, you're too obvious for anything. You fall in at a finger-touch. If you want to be sarcastic you must hide your tools a little better. I can always see you carving out your sarcasm with a bread-knife.'

'I don't see why I should make my women talk differently from real women. How many does one meet who talk cleverly?'

'How many does one meet who are worth writing about at all. Ten? Twenty? Look through fiction. You could count all the great women characters on four hands, on two, perhaps. More than half have come from one man's pen, George Meredith's.'

'But look through history. History proves that there were more than twenty women worth writing about.'

'Not as characters. Only as bits of spectacular dramas, as threads in tapestries too immense to be lifted bodily into a book. The tapestries would not have fallen to pieces without them. They would have been less gorgeous, but would have held together. But the threads taken out of the tapestries would have lost their colour, and been barely beautiful and wholly ineffective.'

'But men say that women who talk cleverly are a bore. They dislike clever women as a rule.'

'Clever men don't. Men don't like women to be clever enough to see through them, but they like a woman with brains enough to appreciate their appreciations.'

'But what am I to do with my women? What am I to make them say?'

'Make them say things to the point. You always keep them at the point of making conversation, your story in the meantime standing deadly still.'

'You are horrid. Don't you think I have any brains, then?'

'I'm sure you have. I never heard anything neater than the way you snubbed the Englishman. But you can't write, Jean, you *can't* write.'

'Everybody does not think with you.'

'You'll never master the first principle of your art-brevity.If you want to say it rains, say it rains, La Bruyere said that. Now you would say, "the cold grey rain fell with a plaintive moan."'

'Well, I don't elaborate when I call you a pig.'

'Perhaps I'm in a bad temper,' said the friend presently.

'Have some tea,' said Jean, 'and we'll discuss that afterwards.'

She lit the little gas-ring on her table, and put a small bronze kettle on to boil. An afternoon tea-table stood by with an equipment of cups, milk, sugar and dainty cakes.

'When I want tea I have to go into the kitchen and make it,' said the friend plaintively, watching Jean with the tiny silver teapot.

'What fun!'

'Fun. I never thought of it in that way. I suppose then you'd call it fun to wear a hat without any trimming, and shoes without any soles.'

'Certainly,' said Jean. 'Immense fun. I'd love to see myself doing it.'

'I believe I could do something if I had everything I wanted. If I had always nice shoes and a little nest of my own, and no worry about money.'

'How you harp on the shoes. I never notice yours.'

'Reason why - I always keep them hidden.' She put her foot forth. 'But see.'

They could scarcely have been shabbier.

'But you don't write with your feet,' said Jean. She felt as if this was a reflection on her for not writing better.

'No, but I could write better if my shoes were nice and comfortable, and vamped, and kidded, and patent-leathered like yours.'

'You *could?*'

Jean put the teapot down, and began suddenly to unfasten her shoes.

'Then try,' she said. 'Just try for a minute. And I'll put on yours without any soles, and your hat without any trimming, and your gloves without any-'

'Fit.'

'And we'll see if it makes any difference to our mighty intellects.'

The friend had small neat feet, and Jean's shoes set them off to perfection. When she had tied the wide silk laces, she stood and stared at them, and pulled her dress up a little.

'Lend me that red silk tea-gown of yours.' Jean produced it from the other room, and helped the friend to slip it on over her dress. It was a beautiful thing, all frills and lace, and warm rich colour, and the friend's dark face seemed to glow out of it with a sudden accession of loveliness.

Jean took up the little black sailor hat, with its narrow ribbon band, and put it on her head, and fastened up the fitless gloves, then began to laugh.

'Now,' said the friend, triumphantly, fastening the bottom button of her tea-gown.

'Well,' said Jean.

'Could you think with those shoes floating about on your feet, and the knowledge that those terrible gloves were your best?'

She drew herself up, looked admiringly over her shoulder, sat down in a wicker chair for a moment, and let her head sink into a luxurious eider-down cushion. Then got up, and trailed about the room, and going to the desk sat down there, took up a carven pen with a gold T nib in it, and began to write:-

Fame came to me in my sleep;
Oh, the sweet, wild, dreamless dreaming!
I looked to the highest steep,
I leapt with a long straight leap,
Till the world was wind beneath me.
I laughed and leapt with the winds and sun,
A god I burst through them one by one.

Far down through sunlight and red-heaped cloud,
The watching world to my footsteps bowed,
Then the sting of a myriad hand-claps broke
On the air like hail, and I laughed and woke.
Just lor a moment's lightning dream,
I leapt to godhead, I ruled supreme.
But the sting of Fame's poisoned arrow glows
In my heart, and the dart will never close.

'I could go on forever,' she said, throwing down the pen. 'Oh, it's disgusting to be poor, to have ten brothers and sisters with tremendous appetites and big minds that require to be educated in the very best manner possible. Do you know, sometimes I sit down and think, and see an endless succession of days of failure, and I feel I can't stand things any longer. Teaching is so horrible. It takes the curl out of your hair, and the backbone from your body, and gives you dirty nails, and a contemptible mental attitude, and a bad temper. My heart nearly breaks sometimes with its weight of wants. I want time, I am getting so old. I want to go away, anywhere, anywhere, into the world. Oh, if I could only go to London, or Paris. I believe I could write there. But here I am good-for-nothing. I can't write about Australia, it doesn't appeal to me. I can't get hold of it. What is there in a town like this to wake one up? Of bush life I know nothing. Colonial though I am, I have never taken my country into my soul, and never will until I get away from it.' After this outburst she sank into the wicker chair again, and let her head fall back into the silk cushions.

Just then a maid knocked at the door with some letters. Jean opened them, and from one a little pink-coloured clip came fluttering to the floor. She picked it up and folded it out.

'A cheque for three guineas for my last little tale,' she said.

If there was any triumph in her heart as she remembered all the friend's disparagement of her work, she did not show it now. Instead she crumpled the cheque up quickly, and pushed it into a drawer, and then went on hastily with the tea making. But there was a gloom on the friend's face that refused to be melted even by tea from that bewitching tea-pot.

'I am thinking,' she said, 'whether I ought not to go and do likewise.'

'You must do what is in you,' said Jean.

'I could write that -like you-for the *Evening Times* if I tried hard enough. It is never a very difficult thing to come down a hill. And three guineas at a time is not to be lightly despised.'

She grew gloomy again, and they drank their tea rather silently.

Over her second cup she revived.

'No, no,' she said, 'I have cut out my way, and I will stick to it.

- *tasks in hours of insight will'd*

Can be through hours of gloom fulfill'd.

'I will not write when I have nothing to write about but reminiscences of lady novelists' books. I will wait. In the meantime I have decided to go up into the bush and teach a family of station children. They want me to go next week. Will you and Monty come and spend the evening with us next Saturday? I have asked a few rather nice people. There will be nothing to eat.'

'I should like to shake you. Yes, I should love to come. But are you serious about going away?'

'Truly.'

'Oh, but what am I to do without you?' blankly.

'There are letters,' said the friend, 'and if it is my criticisms you are thinking of, I promise you to be even more unsparing in black and white than I have been to-day.'

But there was something deeper than a literary kinship in the kiss Jean gave her at parting.

At the door the friend observed, 'Mr Musgrave is coming. Do you often see him?'

'I have met him two or three times lately.'

'And is he as clever as ever?' innocently.

'My hat straight? Good-bye. You have done me good. It is a wonderful outlet for your depression to abuse somebody you like.'

6

The Friend In Black and White

Harrison sat on a stiff chair in a corner of the friend's drawing-room and looked at Jean. Musgrave sat on the little blue sofa beside her, and talked to her. Harrison wondered if Musgrave had forgotten what had happened the other day in Monty's chambers. Musgrave talked and thought of nothing in the world but Jean. His finely cut face was looking unusually handsome to-night. His strong, blue eyes snapped and sparkled. He laughed with a boyish abandon that was fascinating even to Harrison, and he talked with a confidence born of the knowledge that his listeners would laugh when he wished them to laugh, and be grave when he meant them to be grave.

Jean was enjoying herself immensely. She always did enjoy herself here.

She gave a furtive glance round the room. She knew every detail of it by heart, and yet to-night she looked at it wonderingly. It was not even a big room, and it was shabby and worn out almost to the last degree. The sofas had long since parted with their springs, and went down with a horrid rapidity if you sat down on them too quickly. The carpet-pattern had been trodden out of all recognition by big and little feet. The window-curtains were thick with darns. The palms and flowers about the tables were as often as not arranged in empty jam-tins or salt-bottles, cleverly disguised by an artistic younger sister of the friend's. An armchair with a frill round it, had a log of wood in place of one of its legs, and the friend's mother had been bidden to sit in it all the evening to save accidents, in case Musgrave or Harrison should try to alter its position.

Seen in the day-light, 'Poverty' was written on every article in the room, and yet, of all the rooms Jean knew, there was not one with such an electrical atmosphere of gaiety and happiness about it as this shabby little place possessed. There was something deliciously infectious floating about in the air of it. Everybody was brighter here than anywhere else. People talked more brilliantly, laughed more naturally, and found themselves of more importance.

The secret of it was that everybody felt at home. And the people who came there knew well that the passport through that blistering old front-door was neither wealth, nor prospects, nor position. It was brains and human kindness. The friend's mother was a dear little woman with only one gown in the world, a sense of humour, and fingers that loved the feel of the leaves of new books. The father was a dreamy old man with a hundred hobbies, and an abnormally receptive mind. He knew something about everything (except moneymaking, his wife said). Whatever topic was started he had always something interesting to say about it, and he always listened to what anyone told him.

He wandered across the room and drew a chair up to Harrison. 'Do you know anything about Paythorpe's new picture?'

They were lost to the world for awhile.

The mother was deep in discussion with an ugly man who believed that the University was a very much over-rated factor. He brought forward Walt Whitman as the type of man University life would have cramped and spoilt. The mother was a little aghast. She had a respect for Universities, and urged all her sons thither.

The friend was entertaining Monty, who was in love with her, and another man with her brisk bright talk. A younger sister was playing bits of Schumann with a scholarly touch, and an old lady sat near the piano listening happily.

'What a blessed little place it is,' said Jean involuntarily.

'It is,' said Musgrave heartily.

A little quick glow of good fellowship warmed her heart.

She was pleased with him for being so spontaneous, for these people had a warm place in her regard, and she looked at him and smiled.

'You can be very nice sometimes,' she said naively.

'Everyone has his good points,' he said laughing. 'Even I,' in a lower voice.

'I can be horrid enough myself sometimes,' said Jean. She looked at him again. He was sitting near her, and she only had to turn her head a little to do so. A gas light behind shone straight into his face, and it struck her for the first time since she had known him that there was something very kind in the expression of his eyes. Then she remembered that she had never looked so closely at them, for he had turned towards her, and there was not so very much space between their two faces. And then, quite suddenly and before she could look away, he was saying to her in a lowered voice, 'It is quite true. You can be horrid. You were to me when you would not believe me about Miss Macqueen. You were very hard about it, do you know. I showed you plainly how the mistake might have arisen. It was an easy enough thing for her to have misunderstood me. She half acknowledged it herself. Only you, you. Why are you so hard?'

To attack her there, with all those people around, was a bold venture. She quite lost her self-control.

'I am not hard,' she said piteously.

'Not to everybody,' said Musgrave, 'but you are to me.'

He hardly knew whether he had forced that sad shade into his voice, or whether it had come there naturally.

'I don't wish to speak of it,' said Jean, hurriedly.

'Then I will not. Only let me say this. You are wronging me terribly. You are really.'

'How can you say I am hard to you when I talk to you so much,' recovering herself a little.

'You never talk of anything but books.'

'I have heard you say that books are the only things worth talking about.'

'And oneself. There are one or two people to whom one cares to talk about oneself.'

His smile said, 'You amuse me when you try to quibble.' His voice said, 'Don't you think it would be wiser to discuss this?'

'I see no need for that. I don't know why you bring up tonight - and here.'

'I don't think time and place matter as much as people think,' said Musgrave. 'And I have so few chances of talking to you.'

'We talked for over an hour that night you dined with us.'

'About your writing, all the time.'

'I knew it bored you,' hotly. She had not known anything of the sort.

'It did not bore me. I never talk if I am bored. And I always have so much to say to you that no talk could be long enough.' He said this in a perfectly common-place manner, that robbed the remark of any undue flattery.

'If you know I doubt your word, how can you like me?' said Jean.

'I see,' said Musgrave. 'That weighs against me, does it? But then I might reply, how can you doubt my word, and yet like me?'

It was such a terribly audacious thing to say that he held his breath a minute after and wondered what would happen next. But the eyes that looked at him had only wonder in them. 'You are the strangest man I know,' she said, at last. 'And you are right. I do like you.'

'But you do not believe in me.'

His eyes forced hers to look into them. They were steady and grave.

'I - don't know.'

But the pause before the 'don't know,' meant much to him, and he knew she would remember what he had said, and how he had looked. The clatter of cups interrupted them, and he went away to get her some coffee. The friend came hurriedly across the room, and sat down in his vacant seat.

'Jean,' in a whisper. 'For Heaven's sake only have one cup of coffee. I don't believe it will go round. Jimmie drank half the milk, little wretch, and I could only make one potful.'

Jean began to laugh.

'You *funny* things,' she said.

'Indeed, it isn't. It's awful. But I knew Mr Musgrave, or somebody, would ask *you* to have some more, so I thought I'd warn *you*. I don't mind *you.'*

She flew away again.

A little later in the evening, as Jean was chatting with Harrison, the friend's father came along and stopped in front of her.

'Let me get *you* some more coffee,' he said.

'Not any more, thank *you,'* said Jean.

'Oh, do have another cup,' he urged hospitably. Coffee and little cakes made up the supper menu. She had turned to continue her talk with Harrison, and did not notice that he was waiting for a reply. After a minute he murmured, 'Silence means consent,' and picking up her empty cup took it over to the table where the friend stood with the coffeepot.

'Miss Jean will have some more coffee, dear,' he said.

'Let me take it to her,' said Musgrave, who stood nearby, eating one of the little cakes. A desperate look crossed the friend's face. She shook the coffee-pot a little, said 'Wait a minute,' and went out of the room.

In the kitchen there were three boys and a girl, all eating bread and dripping, and talking about the people inside. The friend burst on them suddenly.

'Is there any more coffee at all?' she asked.

'Not a drop,' said the little sister with the long brown hair, 'of course there isn't.'

'Whatever shall I do?'

'Why, wasn't there enough to go round?' asked the boys.

'That Dad went and begged Jean to have some more, and Mr Musgrave is waiting there to give it to her.'

They ceased to eat their bread and dripping, and stared sympathetically at her.

'Why doesn't Dad mind his own business,' they said indignantly.

'Oh, *why* did I ever think of asking anyone to come! I never will again.'

'Y' always say that. Y' ask them all the same though,' said one of the boys.

'I don't know what to do,' despairingly.

'Why didn't you tell Jean not to have two cups.'

'I did.'

'Well, she's a nice one.'

'She must have forgotten. Or perhaps Dad pressed her awfully.'

'Let us pour some hot water on the grains,' said the little sister. 'There's no milk, and she won't be able to drink it, but she won't say anything.'

'That's all I can do,' said the friend.

A few minutes after a cup of coffee was handed to Jean.

She took it absently, and sipped it. It was quite cold, and so exceedingly nasty, and so strongly reminiscent of dirty dish water, that she looked up in involuntary surprise. But across the room she caught the friend's eyes frowning fiercely at her, and at the same time she became aware that heads were peeping at her through the door that opened into the hall. A sudden spasm of remembrance flashed through her.

'I promised not to have any more. They must have faked this up for me,' she said remorsefully. Then she drank every drop of it with an unmoved face. She liked them all the better for it, and though the contrast was extreme between her aunt's elaborate suppers, and this little pitiful attempt at refreshment, she told herself that these evenings were a hundred times nicer than her own. Musgrave, sitting near her, was thinking exactly the same thing. There were no Patriots, and no daffodil satins. A week later, the friend packed her dingy brown box, glossed her black sailor hat with her boots, put a new ribbon round it, and set off in a second class carriage on her journey into an unknown land. She was going to a station out west, and as Jean stood on the platform, and watched the red train lights disappearing through the Redfern tunnel a feeling that was strangely like envy mixed with her genuine depression at the loss of her comrade. The shabby tin trunk, the crowded second class carriage, the tears in the brown eyes, the uncertainty and possible hardships of the position before her, the loneliness, Jean forgot all these, and remembered only that it was a monotonous thing to ride homeward in a railway train with the lights of Sydney flickering none too brightly through the gloom. It was depressing, too, to have no thin, shabby figure coming in near dusk, to throw herself on the study sofa, and tell what she had been doing through the day, or listen to what Jean had to say. Up there in the study with the door shut and locked, they could make fun of people as they pleased; nobody ever interrupted them, and when their laughter floated a way down the staircase nobody came rushing in to see what they were laughing at. At the friend's house it was different, so the friend had come often to the study for rest and confidences, and Jean missed her horribly.

After a time she began, quite unconsciously, to look around for someone to fill the vacant place. Musgrave was nearest, and she began to tell him of the friend's adventures, and how she missed her, and to read him bits of the long fascinating bush letters. And by-and-by the friend dropped out of their conversation, and they found new themes with which to interest themselves.

The friend, in her far country, began to read unwritten things between the wide lines of Jean's letters. The lines of her own were close together, and Jean read and re-read them, and enjoyed them as much as the latest novel, but it seemed that the friend had not the same satisfaction with hers.

'The Wilderness'

'Dear Jean-What shall be said between us here? Your letters are always so clear and so neat; they smell so daintily of violet and other sachets, the tints of your notepaper are always adorable. I am proud, being only a governess on a wild bush station, of getting letters with a thick gold crest on them, and a suggestion of Paris hovering about them.

'And yet-

'Couldn't you, just now and again for the artistic value of contrast, tear a sheet or two out of an exercise book and write very small on it, and not copy, and not mind blots, and forget that I am a long way off, and write to the very bottom of the very last page, and remember that you are Jean, and I am your friend, who knows that you wear high-heeled shoes to make you taller, and dress in blue to deepen the tint of your eyes, and tell me things in a talking voice, as when we are together on the sofa in the study and the gas is not yet lit?

'I don't want to know what the Fresh Air League Ball was like, or what you saw at the theatre, and what you thought of it, or what you are going to see next.

'I want to know what you are thinking, what you are writing, reading. And some nasty things about people that I know for spice. And what you had for breakfast, and what you had for dinner, and what you had for tea, and what anybody says about me.

'It seems to me that all the little common-place things that nobody troubles to tell you are the things you want most to hear when you are away from home. Everybody leaves them for someone else to tell, and I never hear them at all. And I ache for them, the pretty little everyday details of the everyday things that made up my life in Sydney.

'You will notice how fearfully constructed my sentences are. Since I came here I have let rust grow on my old black pen, and my foolscap has hardly a line on it. I meant to write so much too. I only teach for four hours out of the day, so I ought to have plenty of spare time, and yet the days slip by, and slip by, and I write nothing. Nor do I want to write. The bush has taken hold of me. I feel myself growing into its silences, the weirdest, most wonderful silences, and it is enough to look and to think. Somebody said somewhere, "Those whom the gods love ride across an Australian plain at sunset." I ride, and the West is a blood-stained world, deepening, shifting, illimitable, and the grass underfoot is crisp and yellowy, and the world seems as if there was no end to it, and no beginning. A little wind in the face, the stir of clouds overhead, and oneself and one's horse, the only moving things. As I rush through the air with my face to that wonderful sky, I feel my heart beat quicker and quicker, and my brain grow into a trancelike ecstasy, and I believe I mutter, God, God, under my breath. I feel that I have got hold of Him then on the plain, in the wind and the sunset.

'Thoughts like these come rushing through my brain.

'I, petty, cabined, with my body dwelling upon the earth, my soul everywhere.

'I acknowledge no bounds.

'I know no space.

'I fear no time.

'I in myself am time and space, and all boundary lines throughout the universe.

'I have only to sleep or to make myself insensible, to realise the futility of giving any meaning to the word "time".

'For we lay down laws, and we divide time into moments, hours, years, and a moment comes that seems longer than a hundred moments. It may be longer than an hour, or than a year, for what happens in it remains with the watcher when all things else are forgotten. Who shall say it was a minute?

'There are no limits to time and no conformities. With every man it is different.

'There may be laws which fit me, but there are no laws which fit me because they fit other people.

'Or there may be no laws among all the good honest laws which would not become false, and meaningless if applied to me.

'Law is often merely conformity, and merely to conform is to shut the eyes and bar the light of the sun from those dark places where light is needed most. It is to Cut the wings and leave the open stretches of the highland for a dungeon.

'But it is good to find that your own thoughts and conformity will go together.

'You will say that I have been reading Walt Whitman, and ask me if I mean the foregoing for verse. My book of verse will never gain me the bliss I covet as the author of books of verse, to be asked out to dinner by people who could not know me when I was unknown, and to refuse without giving them a reason.

'But you must remember that I am in the Wilderness, among people who are about as literary as the people I meet sometimes at your house, or perhaps I wrong my Bushies a little. I remember Mrs Raymonda and her silvered shoes, and her description of Shakespeare. "He was so very clever, you know." Not even the Bushies would profane the memory of the Immortal god with such an epithet as that. Oh, it sickens me. That posturing, pseudo-intellectual Sydney set, with its Literary Societies, and its wearying, unending chases after the Theories of the Moment, its ignorance, its Aides-de-camp, its Society Women, its Lights of the Medical Profession, and above all, the affability with which one member agrees with another's opinions.

'Thank God there are no literary societies in the bush, no aides-de-camp to read us archaic papers on Horace, no willof-the-wisp theories to be chased and caught, as you value your position in society. Here you can think as you like or not think at all. The gums, and acacias, and rolling sunsets, and strong sweet winds, and great plain stretches, and the horne-paddocks at noon or under the moonlight, these are better than any society for the promotion of intellectual literature. They are thought themselves, and their meaning can never be put into words.

'As for the Bushies, they are adorable, the long, shy, silent creatures, with their green and purple fly-veils, their nervous, uneven walk, their kind, pure, childish eyes, their atrocious "yairs", "sniike", niice day", their tenderness to women and dumb animals, their primeval patriotism, their sturdy democracy. And the young Bushies, the boys scarcely out of their teens with their beards, and their home-made suits, puce neckties, husky voices, hair oil, pumps (as they call their evening shoes), their hidden hoard of unconscious sentiment, their reverence for Rolf Boldrewood. Their bitter contempt for that profound and scurrilous egoist, Max O'Rell-the same Max who fattened on their land with a ready continental smile, and went away and gave the world a string of frothy sarcasms about their tea-drinking and meat-eating, and pitiable drunkenness and antecedents, their deep and undying love for Gordon's "Sick Stockrider", and "How we beat the Favourite". I regard them all tenderly, and never grow tired of watching them.

'It may be that their conversation is at first a little *difficile*. Here is a specimen of one that took place the night after I arrived.

'Bushie - Do you liike the country?

'Me - Well, I have hardly been here long enough to know.

'Bushie - Aeour (I don't know if I have spelt it quite correctly.)

'Me - I am sure I shall like it though, everything is so different from Sydney, and I was deadly tired of Sydney.

'Bushie - Aeour.

'Me (desperately) - I suppose you have been to Sydney.

'Bushie- Yairs [pause].

'Bushie - Do you like horses?

'Me - Oh, I love them.

'Bushie - Can you ride?

'Me - Well, I can canter all the way.

'Bushie - Ca-antering is very ni-ice.

'Me - Trotting is so-er-heavy.

'Bushie - Yairs.

'Me - I think most people prefer cantering, don't you?

'Bushie - Yairs.

'Me - Which do you like best?

'Bushie - Trotting.

'Me (surprised)-Do you? oh well, I would even trot if I could be on horseback as often as I liked. You see, I very seldom have a chance of riding in Sydney. [He shuffles his eyes from one foot to the other.] I live at Paddington. [He lets them raise themselves as high as his hands.] And it would be terribly expensive to keep a horse there. You don't see many good horses in Sydney [brings them up to my face, at once drops them, and looks away under the far chair], except racers, out walking with their jockeys.

'Bushie - Aeour.

'He repeats the eye-drill again and again, but listens attentively to every word I say.

'Well, that was not a very exciting conversation, I grant you, but I give you my word, that it afforded me much more entertainment than a type which you and I have both endured countlessly in town.

'Town man - I like a good yarn with a plot in it. Don't you?

'Me - I really don't know [in a remotely Arctic voice]

'Town man-Came across an awfully good yarn today. A jolly well worked-out thing. It was about a fellow in-er-some place in Queensland, I forget the name of the place, something like-er-Raymondstown, or Raymond's Creek, or-er-Raymond's-er-oh, I forget the name of the place, but this fellow, Smithers, I think he was called, let's see, was it Smithers? no, Smithson, Smeaton, Smithers. Yes, I believe it was Smithers; or else it was Smithson; at any rate, he was on the wallaby out West, and he came across a bag of bones. They were supposed to be the bones of an Aboriginal named [dead pause. Nothing that in any way resembles the name suggests itself to him, and I hope he will now give it up.] I forget his name, but he was the chief of a tribe out on the -those mountains out there. Awfully well worked-out yarn. It was in the-one of these papers here, signed M. or N. I think. You ought to read it.

'The odour of undiluted gum-trees was strong in the Bushie's conversation; no forced essences tampered with its native perfume, so it was enjoyable and fresh, and bush-like and slow.

'But the town-man with his story by an author he could not remember, in a paper whose name he had forgotten, with a plot which he entirely failed to reveal to you, about people whom he could not distinguish, in a place he could not locate, what weariness and depression he aroused!

'The Bush girls are shy, clever, wonderfully deft and domesticated, and consumed with ambitions which they never speak of. One of the things that struck me most about them is their intense fervent desire to improve their minds. They will practise painstakingly day after day for years and years, with no further music lessons than the elementary ones from a hardworked mother. Patiently they wait their chance, which comes sometimes in the shape of a musical governess on an adjoining station, who is perhaps induced to give them a lesson once a month. How they revel in that! And their reading is just as painstaking, and conscientious. History is the special study to which they devote themselves, and between ourselves, Jean dear, if you and I were put through the mill of knowledge of this particular subject with them, we would come out somewhere at the bitter end. Or I; at any rate. If you want to know anything, never ask a graduate.

'But I must tell you, without conceit, that I have learnt a great deal since I came here, learnt and remember. I know now that a Plymouth Rock is a fowl, and not a sheep; that a Brumbie is a wild untamed horse, and nothing to do with a Bushie; that kangaroo-tail soup is an epicurean delicacy; that potted eel is better than the choicest chicken; that you can walk ten miles without seeing a snake; that the dawn is the sweetest time of the day.

'Write to me soon, a long letter, with everything I want to know in it.

'Your friend.'

7

In the Fog

Winter was over, the short delightful Australian winter. The scent of the subtle sweet things deepened in the air. The gardens about Sydney grew fairer and fairer with flowers; millions of roses came out together. Under the gum trees, 'up the country', shining buttercups began to spread a waving golden carpet over the grass of the paddocks and hillsides.

When the moon came to its full that month, somebody at Double Bay, unable to resist any longer the spring's sweet fascinations, gave a moonlight picnic on the harbour.

Jean went singing about the house all that day. She was going, and Musgrave, and Harrison, and Montagu, and the Friend who was home for her holidays, and many others.

A moonlight picnic on Sydney Harbour, with the westerly winds asleep, and the springtime wringing all the hearts of the flowers out on the air in an ecstasy of sweetness; with the little winter months not far behind, and the broiling summer days still well in front, with mosquitoes yet a long way off, and the balmy daytimes dying down to gently tempered eventimes. No wonder Jean sang!

She could not work that day. The thought of the evening was too distracting, for it was the first picnic of the season. She laid out her pens, and her paper, and pretty ink cruet, and sat herself down before her motto, but no line came. Instead only the thought that the band on her sailor hat would not match the blouse she purposed to wear that night, and that she must not forget to change it. And presently she went to do so, leaving pens and paper unused for the day.

She felt a little guilty as she stitched that hatband on.

'I really ought to write to-day. I don't seem to be getting on. I wish now that I hadn't raised that question of evolution in the third chapter. It's frightfully hard to settle. I had no idea how hard it would be. And I can't leave it out for the story hinges on it. I must think when I have time-to-morrow.

She puckered her brows a little, then began to hum' Ma Mie Rosette', and went to find a tie to match her hat-band.

The town never grew dark that day. Before the sunlight faded from the west the moon was round and reddened in the east, and the harbour lay like one vast sheet of perfect glass, with the lights of ships at port, and passing ferry-boats, green lights, and red, and yellow, and the strong white beams of the lighthouse at the South Head, and the silver image of the moon, all mirrored on its surface.

Every now and then the little puffing busy steamboats cut the waters on their way to the harbour's northern shores, and left their smoke-trails on the wind behind them. And now and then a rowing-boat crept out from the shadows round shore with a couple of lovers in it or a family party, middies from the men-o'war, or solitary rowers come to enjoy the fairness of the night. This night had so little to do with sleep. It was a day that buoyed one up with a strange elixir of life, not keen but gentle, and so sweet as to make one glad that one was alive, and that the world was beautiful.

It was just six o'clock as they puffed out briskly from one of the wharves at the Circular Quay, and there was the sun's red ball in the west, and the moon's red ball in the east, one sinking as the other rose.

Harrison, who had found a seat beside Jean, and was trying hard to think of something interesting to say to her, observed at last, 'There will be a fog to-night if the southerly goes down. It has been so warm to-day.'

Jean laughed: then looked grave.

'It will be wet to-morrow-if it rains,' she said.

But for all that she was very friendly to him that evening.

She only laughed at him that once, and did not snub him at all.

They steamed out of the quay, past the grey stones of Fort Denison, turned round by Bradley's Head, and went on to Middle Harbour. The narrow length of The Spit ran out whitely into the water, and its sand shone in the moonlight. Away across the harbour the lights of Manly showed dimly red through the distance. The gums, and acacias, and all the wild things along the wooded shores grew darker and darker as the moonlight deepened, and the sunlight faded away. The city was out of sight now, left here in this long quiet stretch of water all the world seemed to have gone to sleep. On, on, past many famous picnic grounds, past Fig Tree, and Pearl Bay, Quaker's Hat, right up under the Suspension Bridge.

They landed near there, and had *al fresco* high tea in the moonlight.

Harrison ran about a great deal. He filled jean's cup twice with tea. He brought her the salad, and conscientiously found her the salt and the pepper, and the mustard, and was very grave indeed over choosing her some chicken.

And when he sat down near her he looked at her so often that he almost forgot to eat anything himself. Which was a pity perhaps, for he did not often have as good a tea as this before him. But nobody noticed, and he himself was utterly happy.

Only one thing troubled him. He had so little to talk about.

Whenever a silence came between him and jean, he had to rack his brains for something to say. jean, unconscious of this, ate on happily and hungrily, talked to one and another, laughed, watched Montagu and the friend arguing spiritedly over their tea, noticed how pretty the friend looked in her pale, pink blouse, and with that gleam from the fire on her face and hair, and hoped she would care for Montagu; noticed how devotedly Musgrave looked at the hostess's youngest daughter as he brought her some jelly, and remembered that he had talked to that same daughter all the way down in the boat. Then she forgot Harrison, and was silent so long that he was worried exceedingly, for he thought she was waiting for him to speak.

It was some time before any ideas would occur to him.

At last - 'Miss Star did not come to-night,' he said, turning to her.

'No,' said Jean, with a little start, 'she is too young.'

'Miss Star is-er-improving very much in her-er drawing,' said he.

'As if I want to talk about Star at a picnic,' said Jean to herself, indignantly.

But she asked him kindly how his own work was getting on, and she said she was glad when he told her he had sold two pictures that month, and would have five hanging at the Art Society's Exhibition next week.

'You will be quite famous soon,' she said blithely, and Harrison flushed all over with delight.

And after that he was happy for the evening. Even when the hostess gave him a stout old lady in black to take care of, and he saw Musgrave making his way to Jean's side, while everybody rambled about a little in the moonlight, he was happy. He could not ramble in the moonlight though. He had to sit beside his charge, and listen to her while she talked about the harbour, and the quantity of fish in its waters, the terrible price of that fish, how fond her son was of it, and the possibility of Parliament doing something soon to cheapen it.

When he found himself on the steamer again, and still talking fish to his old lady, and saw Jean and Musgrave pass on together towards the stern, it did occur to him that a wiser man than he would perhaps have looked out for stout old ladies on the way down, and reserved the delights of Jean's company for the idle dawdling homeward trip. But he was philosophical, and hoped to walk beside her when they landed at the Quay. At present they were making an aimless lazy cruise about the harbour, passing from one lovely bay to another, rocking a little as they carne opposite the mile of waters between the two great Heads, steaming round the little moonlit islands, just wandering anyway. The moon went under a cloud, and it stayed there for so long a time, and the cloud thickened so that the night began to grow very dark. A sharp chill feeling crept into the air. The south wind had died down slowly, and a mist was creeping over shore and tide. It was light at first but grew greyer and heavier every minute.

The shores became misty and indistinct. Jean and Musgrave looking at each other, and talking, did not notice that the moon had gone and the harbour was wreathed in a thickening fog. Musgrave was talking to Jean about himself. He was telling her of the struggle he had had to make a way for himself at the Bar, and into his story crept incidents of other men, his own opinions of them, tersely expressed.

Jean was strangely interested.

A woman is flattered when a man tells her about himself, and other men; a man is bored when a woman tells him about herself and other women.

'I like listening,' she broke in. 'I like you when you talk to me as you would to a man.'

'Or as a woman thinks a man talks to a man,' said Musgrave. She turned her head to look round into his face, and as she did so a little gust of wind caught the gossamer flying loosely from her hat and blew it right away over her head. Musgrave sprang up to catch it for her, but it was clinging to a notch of wood at the edge of the roof, just out of his reach.

He jumped onto the seat, and throwing an arm loosely round the nearest post, leaned out a little, and stretched one hand up to grasp the rail.

Just then, he leaning so, there rang through the boat a heavy thudding sound, as of some great body bumping violently against it. Then came a long shudder that seemed to shake the steamer from end to end. Then another awful bump. And then, for a minute, the fog again, and silence.

Jean sprang to her feet. 'What is it?' she cried.

Everywhere the denseness of the fog baffled the eye and hid all things save those that were very near. The boat was creaking and shuddering still. Everybody was rushing wildly towards the stairs.

The silence ended. Through the fog came the sound of voices, men's voices, loud and hoarse, and now and then a woman's treble.

'What is it?' she said again.

Suddenly she discovered that Musgrave was no longer beside her. The seat next to her was empty. She rushed to the side, and looked over. They were on the upper deck of the steamer, and the ledge outside the railing was a very narrow one. She put her hands out, and felt all along the seat; and even stretched her arms out over the railing that formed the seat's back, and felt about in the air. Fog, fog, everywhere, thick, and deluding, but no sign of Musgrave.

She called him; softly at first, then louder. When she found he did not answer, some strange tone crept into her voice.

'Where can he be?' she whispered. She called to him again and again, he did not answer. Then in a moment a great fear seized her. That great shaking, whatever it was, had dislodged him from the post he was holding to so carelessly, and had cast him away out into the fog-wreathed waters.

At this moment he was out there, drowning perhaps, and all the people were talking at the other end of the boat, and nobody but she knew what was happening.

Her gloves were off, and her nails began to cut into the tender flesh of her palms. She tried to move, to cry out, but for the minute she seemed to have lost all control of herself.

A nightmare spirit seemed to bind her lips, and petrify her will. She could not even breathe naturally. Her mouth was open, and her eyes, but her breath came hardly, and her heartbeats were terrific.

She would have recovered some control of herself in another minute perhaps, but while she stood there, all white and aghast-looking, someone came clambering up the outer side of the boat, leapt the railing, and jumped lightly to his feet beside her.

It was Musgrave.

'We ran into the *Rubberside,*' he said, a little out of breath. 'It shook me right off my hold, and nearly broke my neck. I caught at the edge of the old stairway outside there, my feet were in the water, and - Jean - my God - What is it?'

She was swaying towards him, and as he caught her in his arms to save her from falling, weakly she whispered in a little gasping way, 'I thought-you-were-dead,' and let her head fall forward against his breast.

Musgrave felt the little babyish curls stirring beneath his breath. For a moment he held her and was silent. He held her to him and heard his own, strong heart-beats.

Somewhere-worlds away, it seemed to him, there were voices, men's and women's, all talking together, agitated, some of them, and some calming and reassuring.

'There's nothing in the world to be afraid of.'

He heard somebody say that. He wondered whose voice it was, thought about it, and decided it was the captain's. Then somebody else said plaintively, 'Now do go on with the picnic;' and he ascribed that to the hostess's youngest daughter. Then somebody laughed, because somebody else had cried.

And then suddenly he seemed to realise what this moment meant to him. This golden marvellous moment, strayed into his life through a fog, and a collision. He realised that Jean was in his arms, that her head lay against his breast, and that his safety was of strange account to her.

'Jean,' he whispered.

She was silent. He fancied that she trembled a little. He waited for a while, then he whispered again 'Jean,' and tried to see her face.

'Were you frightened about me? You thought I was drowned perhaps? What did you think? You were frightened. You were frightened for me. Jean, can you hear me?'

'Yes.'

'Oh, my heart, my heart, I love you.'

And he put one hand under her chin, and turned her face a little, and caught one brief glimpse of her eyes.

'Jean, Jean, tell me, tell me. You love me.'

Her head fell back a little, and all the beauty of her face was under his gaze, the eyes with a strange new look in them. The little babyish curls of hair, the pure soft skin, the tender half-smiling mouth.

'You love me,' said Musgrave.

'I didn't know,' said Jean, childishly. She caught her breath in a little sob. 'My saint, my saint,' he was whispering.

He bent his head nearer, nearer. And then, through the fog, two lovers kissed each other for the sweet first time.

8

The World is Round

'Aunt Elizabeth is putting on her very best lace cap,' said Jean. 'She knew your father when she was a girl, you know.' It was the day after, and they stood together in the drawing-room.

'She approves of me then?' holding her hands in his, and looking at her with a tenderness that completely altered his expression.

'She says the Chief Justice would go into dinner at Government House after the Admiral. Like Star, she has a respect for the Bar. Star told a girl at school who tried to bully her, "My brother's a barrister, and a barrister's nearly a policeman" '

But there was a nervous note in her laugh.

'You are thinking of something,' said Musgrave, watching her. 'What are you thinking of?'

He almost forgot what he had asked her in the wonder of the thought that she would answer him henceforth whatever he asked her.

'I don't know,' she said.

She looked down at her hands in his.

'Tell me,' said Musgrave.

'It isn't anything,' said Jean.

'Tell me.'

'Perhaps you won't like it.'

'There is nothing I wouldn't like if you looked at me like that.'

She looked away.

'To think that you are mine,' said Musgrave. 'Oh to think of it, to think of it, Jean, look at me. What colour are your eyes, Jean?'

'I don't know,' said Jean.

'Grey, are they? Or blue? Such sweet dove's eyes.'

'But that's horrid,' said Jean. 'It reminds me of milk and water.'

'Not the doves I mean. You have never seen them. Wait till you come with me.'

'I am sure I heard somebody coming.'

'I didn't. What were you going to tell me? Sit there and let me kneel beside you. Now you are my saint, little Saint Jean. Is it your pale hair that makes you look like a little saint? ... Tell me what you were going to say.'

'I was going to say-at least-well, I don't want to be engaged to you.' She looked and saw the colour going straightway out of his face. The hand round hers trembled.

'What do you mean?'

She had never known before, that there could be a tremor in that voice. She would like to have paused, and thought of it, but she dared not.

'I mean-not in the world's way. I mean I don't want everyone to know. Don't look like that. That's all I mean.'

'Is that all?' He was breathing heavily still.

'Do you mind?' she asked him. 'It is because of my book. I would like to finish it first.'

'Your book.'

'The one I am writing.'

'Oh ...'

That book, that poor little book of hers! He had forgotten it for a while.

'I want it to come out, and be a failure or a success before - everybody knows.'

'You have not given it up then?'

'Given-it-up?'

'I mean, you are writing at it still?'

'I would sooner give up' - a long pause - 'anything.'

'Meaning me,' said Musgrave.

'You are - newer,' said Jean.

'That is the first time I have had that epithet applied to me,' said Musgrave. 'I don't know that it suits me.'

'It does,' said Jean. 'You have a good deal of that bandbox look about you that is so much in fashion now with men.'

'I like the way your eyes crinkle up in the corners, Jean ... But about this. I, like every man, would like everybody to know, and at once.'

'And I, like any woman, can't see what difference it will make.'

It was a good many days before Jean was able to write again. Everything seemed to have twisted itself out of its ordinary course, to have wandered into a vein of golden light, so bright as to blind at first.

She wondered at herself sometimes. Her love for Musgrave had strange points about it. She was always wishing she could know how other girls felt. There were times when, while he was away from her, she felt as if she almost disliked him. She would say to herself sometimes when she knew he was coming, 'Do I want him to come to-day?'

And yet when he had come and she was in the room with him, and he was talking to her in that fine voice of his, or holding her hands, and telling her the secret things all lovers tell each other, the look in her eyes would have no shadow of doubt in its depths. His personality overwhelmed her. It was only when she was away from him that she could doubt herself.

As for the old story about Elsa Macqueen she put it resolutely away from her, and grew to believe in Musgrave absolutely. One day some weeks after, she came down to him in the drawing-room with a very weary look on her face, and a tremendous inkstain on her second finger. She elected to sit on a chair a long way away from Musgrave, and to look as depressed as the peculiar arch of her lips would allow.

'I can't bear to talk to people while they walk about,' she said petulantly. Musgrave's wanderings had evidently the intention of ending in the vicinity of her chair. When she said that, his face fell, and he went back to the sofa. He said nothing.

'What is the good of coming if you won't talk?' said Jean next.

'I thought you did not want to talk to me,' said Musgrave. She looked under her eyelashes, and saw that he looked sombre.

'Of course I am always horrid,' she said. The 'I' sounded like 'you.'

'You are fractious,' said Musgrave, quietly.

She started a little, looked at him. Then leaned her head despondently against the back of her chair, and looked away.

'I am tired,' she said.

Musgrave came and sat on the arm of her chair. He put one arm round her, and kissed her hair.

'I am sorry,' he said, 'little one, I am sorry. Tell me, does anything worry you? You're not fractious, then. You're worried.'

'I can't write,' she said. 'I can't write one other word.' Her voice was despairing, and her eyes filled with tears.

If Musgrave smiled, his face was quickly grave again. 'That is very hard,' he said. 'But it will pass. I know the feeling, but the good hour will return.'

'But I don't know what to do with them.'

'With whom?'

'The people. I want to kill a man and I can't. I don't know how to, and he must die. He has to die.'

'I'm a bloodthirsty wretch. Suppose you let me see what I can do.'

'You! Why you wouldn't trouble yourself with it.'

'Jean! Don't say that. Trouble for you?'

'But would you really?' twisting round to look at him.

'I would kill twenty men for you,' solemnly, , and as cruelly as you please.'

'Yes, it must be cruelly. He has been a terribly bad man, and he must have a bad ending. I thought of smallpox, or leprosy.'

Her face was so soft and pensive that Musgrave laughed out right.

'You little soft sweet child,' he said.

Epithets like those made him forget so utterly the Jean who had despised him, and kept him aloof from her so persistently. 'Let me tell you then. Ah, but I forgot that you don't know what colour your eyes are.'

'If I didn't know you better, I should say that you were a little irrelevant.'

'I flatter myself that I am never that. Are you learning to follow my connections? This last for instance.'

'I can't see any meaning in it at all.'

'You would if you could look into your eyes as I am looking.'

'You think that I might look at other men as I look at you.'

'I think that other men might look at you as I look at you.'

'Well.'

'It would be bad for them, poor wretches.'

'Nothing's proved; said Jean.

'And the only way to secure them safely would be to let them know you belong to me.'

'Sometimes one is allowed to live for oneself,' said Jean. 'And surely one's own engagement is a matter that should be settled without consideration of outside people.' She gave a little shudder. 'Engagement is a horrid word,' she said.

'I quite agree with you,' said Musgrave. 'I have a substitute for it that pleases me far better.'

He was standing behind her, and he bent her head back till he could whisper in her ear.

'To be married,' he said in a low voice.

'That is years off,' said Jean in a very much lower voice.

'How many years?'

'I have not thought yet.'

'Jean! Jean! Ah, the little laughter-marks at the corners of her eyes!' He laid three fingers lightly on her forehead, and went softly and slowly round the outline of her face with them, passing lightly over her cheek and underneath her chin. His eyes softened wonderfully.

'Little Saint Jean,' he said, 'I give in to you. Have your own way. When you give me permission I will let everyone know that you belong to me, but till then I will try and moderate the pride of my looks.'

'It is good of you,' said Jean. 'As soon as my book comes out, I have a fancy that perhaps people might think - I - if they knew that we were engaged- might think that I wrote it from my own - love - story.'

'It shall come out first,' said Musgrave.

'I quite follow your argument. After all, what does anything in earth or heaven matter as long as you have kissed me.'

But he would have liked to tell Harrison nevertheless.

'So what am I to do?' asked Jean.

'Will you show me your manuscript?'

'Oh, I don't know.'

'But I can't help you with it unless I see it.'

'But I couldn't bear to have you reading it where I could see your face.'

'That is easily overcome. Let me take it home with me.'

'It is so heavy.'

'I daresay I shall manage to stagger under its weight.'

'And so badly written, you mustn't notice the writing.'

'Copperplate was invented for solicitors' clerks, dear child.'

'And you must promise one thing.'

'I promise.'

'That you won't tell me what you think of it.'

'Very well.'

He kept his promise.

A week later he brought back the manuscript, which proved to be a most important looking affair, written in a spidery hand on long thick sheets of foolscap. It was already far beyond the length of the average three-volume novel, and yet the end of it was nowhere in view.

'Have you read it?' said Jean.

'Yes.'

'And - it - I mean was it -is it- What did you think of it?'

'I promised not to tell you.'

'I knew you would think it was awful. Is it so very?'

'Not so very. But-'

'But it disappointed you very much.'

'Not at all. It did not disappoint me in the least. There are one or two little things, though, that I would alter. In the first chapter for instance.'

'Oh, I hate it,' said Jean, suddenly. 'I am so utterly tired of it. And to begin to alter the first chapter ... Altering is such horrid work.'

'Let me alter it for you then. I have planned out an original and seemly death for your villain, and I see a way to a unique denouement for you, if you care to hear it.'

She listened while he told her his idea. 'I like that,' she said. 'I like it very much.'

'If you will lend me your manuscript for a week or two I will read it through again, and jot down a rough draft of what I have proposed to you.'

'Oh, if you only knew how glad I shall be to get rid of it for a while. I never have any real rest now. I always feel that I ought to be working away at it. I think that when you start to write a book you deliberately hang a sword of Damocles over your head. It becomes such an awful responsibility.'

'And you are not to have responsibilities. What am I meant for? What is the good of me? You are to make use of me, Jean, do you hear?'

'But I would not like anyone to know you helped me,' said Jean.

'Nobody shall know,' said Musgrave.

It was late in December when they had that talk. Early in January, Jean and Star went away for a few months to the Blue Mountains, the favourite recruiting ground of Sydney girls in search of Roses.

And Musgrave kept possession of the manuscript. Jean never mentioned it in her letters. She seemed to revel in her deliverance from it, and he began to feel that it was really in his hands. He told himself though that he must be very careful. He read it through three times from beginning to end with several weeks between each reading; but his first impression never altered, never softened in the least. At last he set to work on it. Their engagement might be announced as soon as it was published; so the sooner the better.

In November of that same year the world was buzzing over a new book, by a new author.

It was called

THE WORLD IS ROUND

by Jean Melton Burnes

9

In Which Musgrave's Hand Is Forced

Musgrave was in his chambers smoking and reading Fry on 'Specific Performance', an afternoon some three days after Jean's book appeared, when Harrison came up to see him. The westerlies were fierce and enervating, and to them Musgrave ascribed the wanness of Harrison's face, and the paleness of his complexion. There were dark circles under his eyes, and his shoulders stooped even more than of yore, and yet his eyes were full of brisk light, and his face had a sort of secret gladness about it.

'You're not well,' said Musgrave.

'It's this damnable weather,' said Harrison. Musgrave stared.

'Harrison,' he said, 'where have you been? Such language from a youth of your age-'

'Don't be a fool, Musgrave. You're a big man now, you know, and when you're a fool you're a big fool.'

Bitterness was a strong flavour of this speech, and Musgrave was somewhat astonished.

'Your cynicism's astray, sonnie,' he said. 'A big man can never be a big fool. Have a cigar.'

Harrison took one in silence.

'You're right about the weather,' went on Musgrave. 'Damnable is the only word for it. I'm not sorry you've taken a cuss word or two into your vocabulary. One must break out somehow, and they're better for you than whisky.'

'They're cheaper,' said Harrison. 'One can't break out into anything very solid on a pound a week and a poor mother.' He was holding a cigar between his fingers, and he seemed to be inspecting it critically.

'Flor di Havas,' said Musgrave.

'Yes?' His voice was apathetic. He kept on looking at it.

'Match?' asked Musgrave, throwing him his match-box.

Harrison caught it, took a match out slowly, lit it, then let it burn down till the flame was at his finger-tips.

'He has something on his mind,' said Musgrave to himself.

Suddenly Harrison threw away the match, and rising, walked over to the mantelpiece, and laid the cigar and match-box there neatly side by side.

'Aren't you going to smoke?' said Musgrave. Harrison turned round.

'No, not yet. I say Musgrave,' he blurted out, his broad Scotch accent coming out suddenly in strong evidence, his r's multiplied exceedingly, 'You were wrong, after all. That's really what I came for. You were that wrong about Miss Burrrenes. You know I suppose that her name is in evvrabody's mouth. Evvrabody's talkin' of her buke and I have just come from readin' it. It's a fine thing, I tell ye, verra fine.'

Musgrave hadn't time to reply before Harrison went on again with-

'Yes, ya said to me in these verra words "She'll never be anna thing, neverr, neverr, neverr." , Musgrave's cigar began to go out.

'Ya said, "She's not as much literary abeelity as the poker." The cigar grew cold.

'Ya said, "And not as much oreeginality."

He was getting more and more excited, and Musgrave's face-which was always too hard a riddle for him to read - escaped him in its flying changes.

'Ya said, "She has no style, no matter." Ya said, "She will neverr du annathing, neverr, neverr, neverr, neverr.", Musgrave felt as though all the windows in the room were shut.

'An' I've come to tell ya, Musgrave, that for all ye're bigness, ye're briefs and ye're top hats, ye're none so clever as ya think. An, ya were far enough wrong that day. Ya thocht ye'd only to speak the word, and ye'd it all pat and spick. Mind ya, I maself-before God-never thocht 'twas in her to du it. Oh, I freely own I never thocht it. But never did I go so far as you, Musgrave, and ye're a big man, or so ya think.'

He threw his head back, and burst into a boyish laugh, spontaneous and hearty.

'What a sell for ye!' he said; his Scotch set queerly on his slang, but the bitterness had all vanished from his voice.

'There's none so glad as I am,' he said. 'It's all a revelation to me; but, for her sake, I'm glad a thousand times that ya're so far in the wrong as a creetic. Nobody must ever take your judgment again, eh?'

All this time Musgrave had not spoken one word. It seemed to him that he had kept the longest silence he could ever keep in a lifetime.

Harrison went on blithely with his 'rubbing-it-in'. So many a time had Musgrave snubbed and made little of him that this one time of his for retaliation was not likely to be lightly despised by him.

'Ye're better at writin' books than at creeticisin' maybe.'

'Verra possibly.' There was a conceited look about him that made Musgrave's blood seethe and boil.

'You fool,' he said, under his breath.

'Y' always thocht I had no brains, and ya treated ma opinions like dirrt. Whose are the dirrt this time?'

Then began a struggle in Musgrave's mind. An impulse, all but irresistible, took hold of him. To strike out Harrison's unbearable conceit at one blow; to tell the truth, and right himself to his proper position. To have Harrison of all men standing there with that odious wise look in his eyes, chuckling to himself, and making up his mind, as only a Scotchman can do, that this man who had failed in one thing was a failure all through-it was unbearable, it made him writhe.

'Ya said-'

'Harrison,' said Musgrave, catching at his old withering voice, 'For God's sake, shut up.'

'Not at all,' said Harrison, who had not enjoyed himself so much for many a day, and who had probably never before had the piquant satisfaction of kicking an enemy three times in succession.

'Then clear out.'

Harrison chuckled again.

'Evrrabody makes a mistake sometimes,' he said, consolingly, 'Still, it's strange that ah should ha been a better judge of Jean than yu.'

Musgrave started violently. Then he turned very white. 'Remember of whom you speak,' he said, in the tone he would have used to an offending dog.

'I meant Miss Burrnes,' said Harrison, reddening fearfully. 'Ya needn't spik like that.'

'I need,' said Musgrave, in precisely the same key. 'Miss Burnes is engaged to be married to me. You can have nothing to do with her Christian name.'

'*What?*' said Harrison.

'What I said.'

'Engaged - to be married - to you?'

'Yes,' curtly.

'When? When was it - did it happen?'

'We have been engaged for several months now.'

Musgrave went to the mantelpiece and knocked his pipe on it. He could not, absolutely could not, look at the face of the man beside him. In one minute it had changed from the face of a young man, lined perhaps, but young still, to the wan, sick misery of despairing age. It was whiter than his own, and the mouth was trembling.

'You let me say all that and never told me.'

'It doesn't matter, Harrison. It's of no account.'

'You let me crow over you about her.'

'Well, I was wrong. Yes, yes, I was wrong. I'll eat my words if you like. I didn't know what she could do. You were more in the right than I. I'll eat my words. I'll acknowledge I'm no critic. You can enjoy the knowledge. I was mistaken in her-'

'Musgrave!'

'What?'

He looked up. Harrison's eye went through him suddenly like a microscopic spier of his soul. His face twitched. He tried to turn his head carelessly away, but seemed to have lost the power. He and Harrison stood looking silently into each other's faces.

And then,

'*You wrote that book,*' Harrison was saying in a low voice. And it seemed that, in his confusion, he had lost the knowledge of how to fence.

10

'Anywhere, Anywhere-'

Harrison was alone in his room. It was three hours now since had had left Musgrave, but the misery was as marked as ever on his face. He tried to reason with himself. After all, why should it matter so much to him if Jean was false - a hypocrite-untrue at the core? if Musgrave had no sense of honour? Nobody in the world would know of it except themselves, and him. If the world was gulled, it was not in any detrimental way. No unfair advantage was taken of it. It would have read the book just as eagerly if Musgrave's name had been on the title page.

And yet-

'To think she could do it,' was always the end of his attempt to reason with himself. Musgrave had tried to show him that he exaggerated the affair, but had tried vainly.

'She belongs to me, and I to her,' he said. 'I have the right to help her as I will. Surely she has the right to accept that help.'

'Oh no, no,' said Harrison feverishly. 'It's all wrong, I tell you. It's all wrong, Musgrave and you know it.'

'If we have taken the world in, it is the world's fault. Besides, have we taken the world in? I very much doubt if that is what we have done. I was at liberty to withdraw my name from the book. Every author has the right to do that.'

He wondered within himself why he should stay and argue so with Harrison.

'It's not that,' said Harrison. 'It's not that.'

'What is it then?'

'It's this; ye're wrong, and you know it. To do a thing when ye know it's a sin, is a sin.'

'Sin,' said Musgrave. He was recovering himself now. 'Sin! After all,' speaking half to himself, but letting Harrison hear him. 'It's only you, and you were always a fool.'

And when Harrison left him, he was reading Fry again. Or, at any rate, he seemed to be reading it.

Harrison went to his window now, and threw it wide open.

It was seven o'clock, and the sun was setting with all the gorgeousness of an Australian sunset, beyond the University and its buildings. The outlines of the city's buildings were softened into misty beauty, as of heavenly architecture, beneath the shadowy, purple-and-gold-tinted haze of the evening. Away at the horizon's edge the lines of the Blue Mountains ran darkly along the sky.

Harrison's room was at the top of a four-storey lodging-house; he could see from it right across the city, east and west. Could see the gleam of green where the beautiful Botanic Gardens, with their wealth of tropical flowers and shrubs, sloped down to the water's edge. Could see, too, the masts of the shipping round the quay, and the smoke of the little ferry-boats crossing and recrossing with their evening loads of passengers. And what he could not see he could remember. He had not been five years in this fair South Sea city without taking into his soul the full measure of its beauty at sunset time, at dawn, or under the perfect, speckless turquoise of a summer sky at noon. He knew the city in and out; and the harbour; and the country for miles round. At first he had seemed to see a certain crudeness in Australian nature, and Australian art. The chill feeling that something very new gives one, had attacked him; and depressed him; and his soul had sickened for the sight of the ruined castles, oak-trees, cathedrals of the old world, things grown noble with the ages of accumulated emotions that have been spent on them. But the new life, and all the new conditions of it, had crept into his susceptible individuality very quickly, and he had grown to look with appreciative, if not loving, eyes on the things that faced him here.

He stood and watched the floating fiery castles, burning lakes, golden rivers, amethyst seas, that the sun in setting had pictured on the Western sky, and he saw in a brief vision, that the world was immense, was practically unending. Compared to those immeasurable sky-lands, what were Jean, Musgrave, and himself? How much of the world did they occupy? He, one unit in it, was sickening his soul just for one such another unit. Looking up at the sky, for a moment he was taken out of himself with the strange suggestion of space and infinity that the sunlit clouds were building there to-night. Away, away, away, those golden boul-ders were rolling, changing, deepening, melting into one another, and opening vistas that seemed to stretch right back through the very sky, and still to go back, and back, and back, into infinity.

'Only a speck on the world's surface,' he said. 'If I am blown away, what matter?' He got up and walked about his room. A heap of canvases had their faces turned to the wall, and he lifted them, and turned them round, and looked at them. There was one, a likeness of his mother, that he had drawn years ago, and exhibited in a little local exhibition in Scotland. He remembered the pride of his family when they had gone in their best dresses to stand before that picture, and admire it with the important consciousness that the painter of it was 'just our Jamie'. He remembered how he had often scratched his face, when a little boy, against the great old-fashioned cornel ian brooch, with little sharp gold settings, that figured so conspicuously in the quaint old mother's portrait. He looked at it for a long time. And somehow, as he looked, there came into his head the memory of himself, a little lighthaired boy, with bare legs and sandy hairs on them, freckles, and a big mouth, being whipped by his father for something he had never done, whipped with a horse-whip, heavily, and unsparingly. He had scratched his face against his mother's brooch that night. She had come to him in his little bedroom, and drawn his head against her breast, and cried with him. She had said no word, for she was a Scotchwoman, and a wife, as well as a mother, but he had felt that she was sorry for him, and all his heart had gone out to her in love. She had kissed him then. She had kissed him on the railway station the day he left his home to seek his fortune in this new land; and since then no one had remembered that under his old-fashioned Paget beat a heart; until that day when Star had kissed him in the park, under the figtrees.

He put the canvas back suddenly, took his hat, and went out.

He had had no tea, but he did not think of that. He walked on and on until he reached the house he was seeking. He went straight up to the door, rang the bell, and waited. When the servant came he asked if Miss Star was at home, and if he could see her, and gave his card, and went gravely into the drawing-room, and sat down to wait till she should come. Not until the door opened, and Star was in the room, did he realise that he had no excuse whatever for this strange visit, that he had nothing ready to say to her. Star came in with a rush, a little houri in white soft muslin, with a wreath of dark bright-red carnations resting against her fair pretty hair, and a bright colour in her little cheeks.

'Goodness,' she said, seeing Harrison. 'Whatever do you want me for?'

Harrison stood up and shook hands with her. She thought this a strange thing of him to do, for he had seen her only a few hours back at drawing class.

'He needn't have shaken hands again,' she said to herself.

Then he looked at her and said lamely, 'How are you getting on.'

'Me?' said Star in astonishment. 'Why, I'm all right of course. You saw me this afternoon.'

She looked at him with inquiring eyes, and he met her look stupidly. She waited for him to say something. He did not speak. She gave a little twitching touch to her wreath, fidgeted, wondered what he had come for, and at last burst forth, 'I'm having a party. All the girls are waiting for me.'

A party! So that was the reason of the short-sleeved muslin, the filmy lace, and the carnations in her hair.

'An' auntie will be wondering. An' don't you want me for anything at all?'

He did not answer. He still stared stupidly.

"Cos if you don't, I think I'll have to go. I've got to be blind man, and they're all waiting to tie me up.'

She stood on one foot, and rubbed the other impatiently against it. 'I'll tell auntie, shall I? Or Jean?' She was moving towards the door.

'No, don't,' said Harrison, 'it does not matter. I did not know you were having party. But it does not matter.'

'I'll bring you a piece of my birthday cake to school to-morrow.' Perhaps some thrill of feeling stirred in her, a feeling she could not understand.

'Thank you,' said Harrison.

'Jean made it. It's got pink things on it, and little yellow almonds. Jean stuck them in. She's lighting the fairy lamps now for our supper table, and Mr Musgrave is helping her. I won't forget. A piece with a whole lot of pink on it, eh?'

'Yes,' said Harrison.

'I'll bring it to-morrow. You can eat it when Miss Gabie's not looking. Well, I'll have to go now.' She held out her hand to him and said good-night.

'Good-night, Miss Star,' said Harrison: he held her little hands in his for a minute, and looked at her, a long, strange look, gentle, kind, and sad.

He knew now that it was the thought of that day when Star had cried, and kissed him under the fig-trees that had brought him to her to-night.

But to-night there was a party.

Her hand was fidgeting to get away from his. He stooped his head and kissed her little wrist. And then he was out in the street, and Star was flying back four stairs at a time to her deserted little girl guests.

He went back to his lodgings, and shut himself in his room.

It was quite dark now. Only one small star showed its face to him through his window. It watched him narrowly. It saw him sit down by his table, and lay a little hypodermic syringe in front of him. Watched him handle it, and prepare it for his use. Saw him push back his coat sleeve, and bare his arm, and take the soft part of the flesh between his thumb and forefinger, and push the needle in awkwardly with the three back fingers. In a minute it saw him draw it out gently, and rise and go towards the window, and throw the syringe with unnatural strength right into the midst of a pond that had collected in a vacant piece of land some hundreds of feet away. It met his glance as he looked straight up at it, and- knew it could never fathom the look that was on his face just then. It saw him sink into his chair, lean his arms on the table, and let his head fall forward on to his arms. There was only one little quick groan. He was dead almost before his head rested on his arms. The syringe rusted at the bottom of the pond. Nobody noticed the tiny needle prick on his arm. It was too small for notice, and the doctors never knew the truth. Only Musgrave guessed. He had been with Harrison when he had taken the poison from the snake, and he had always known what could be done with it.

11

Was It Hard to Tell

There was a cloud on Musgrave's face, even though Jean sat on the hearth-rug, with her head against his knee.

'How happy we are together,' she said softly. 'And I used almost to hate you once.'

She laid her cheek against the hand that was round her neck. 'Do you think anyone could be as happy as we are? People say that no one ever yet had all they wanted, but I can honestly say that at this minute I haven't one want in the world. Not one. I have my book, and a little shaft of success and the prospect of more to come. And you.'

'You put me in my right place,' said Musgrave, bitterly. 'You are right to put me last.'

She twisted her head round, and stared at him with astonished eyes.

'That is not nice of you,' she said at last, with a shade of coldness in her voice.

'I am not nice,' said Musgrave.

'What is the matter?' said Jean.

She moved away a little from him. He leaned. his head in his hand, and half-closed his eyes. His forehead was shaded, but his mouth was unhidden, and she was struck suddenly with the expression of it. It was drawn, worried, and absolutely miserable.

'What is it?' she asked.

She still stood away from him, but she was asking herself would she go to him, kneel by him, and look into his eyes, when he turned and looked at her.

'Come here.' His voice was not above a whisper. He held her in his arms, and bent his face upon her hair.

'Jean.'

'Yes.'

'Put your arms round me.'

She obeyed him.

'Do you love me?'

'Yes.'

'Better than anyone in the world?'

There was a strange schoolboy element in Musgrave as a lover.

'There is no *better*. I don't love anyone in the same way I love you. As I love *you* I love nobody.'

'How can she?' His whisper was low, and just ruffled her hair, but she heard it.

'I don't know,' she said archly.

'You mean you don't know me.'

'Why do you say that?'

'You don't. You think me one man when I am fifty others, when you disliked me you knew me better than you do now. Now you idealise me.'

'I don't idealise you,' said Jean. Her eyes looked straight into his. 'I never idealised anyone yet. I am not amiable enough to idealise anybody. I believe I know you thoroughly. I suspect you're more than a little obstinate, and you can have a rather cruel disregard of people's feelings at times. You have told me yourself that you have never met a man yet to whom you did not feel yourself intellectually superior, so I suppose you must be what people call conceited. You come nearer to saying everything you mean than to meaning everything you say. You can be more bitter than anyone I know. You are over-hasty in your judgments; and undeniably captious in your opinions on things literary. I would accept your praise unconditionally but not your blame. And then you have a contempt for far too many people. You shut your eyes to their good points. I know you say to yourself, of all my friends, what can she see in them? You're obstinate. I said that. Well, you're very obstinate. Not to me, though. Never to me. Could you be cruel? Could you persecute anyone with a grudge you had against them? Could you be very much in the wrong, and utterly refuse to acknowledge it? I don't know, I don't know. And yet- and yet-I love you, my own boy, I love you *just as you are.*' She looked up at him, looked long and deeply into his eyes, as she looked, her own softened, drooped, and filled with tears.

'My own soul. Little Jean, little Jean ... Ah, the beast I am, the brute.'

There was a silence.

'You have said something like that before,' said Jean. 'Have you ever murdered anyone?'

'No.'

'Have you ever robbed anyone, no? Or ground anyone under foot, till they actually died?'

'No.'

'Then that's all,' she said, and threw her arms round him, and held him tightly. She leaned her head against his heart, and let the strange sweet overpowering feeling of his strong personality surge over her at its will.

'You baby. You child. Oh, my small, sweet, lovely child... '

They stood together so for several long minutes. 'Jean.'

'Yes?'

'I want to tell you something.'

'Tell me then.'

'Keep your arms round me.'

'Tell me.'

'Do you know what I did to-day?' His voice began to quicken. 'I betrayed the confidence of the dearest thing in the world to me. I betrayed your secret.'

Jean stared.

'I - Harrison, - he knows - about the book.'

'What?' She drew herself away from him, and his arms fell limply at his side.

'Yes, he came to me to-day. He was looking horribly seedy and down-in-the-mouth, but I saw there was something behind his depressed looks. Then he began after a lot of shuffling to talk about your book. He teased and twitted me like a fool, threw up a lot of old silly nonsense in my face, and was blind to all my hints for him to clear out. I stood it a long time. Oh, I was martyr-like in my patience. But he went too far. I believe I told him to leave my chambers, and then - I don't know how it happened - he looked at me suddenly, looked, looked, looked, and then he said to me, "Musgrave, you wrote that book." '

'What? What did you say?'

'Nothing.'

'Nothing?'

'Not one word - until a long time afterwards.'

'But he will think that you really wrote it.'

'I seemed to lose my head. I- I- I- Good God, am I going to lie again?'

His face was perfectly livid. Jean's own went white at the sight of it.

'Jean! Jean!'

'I am a liar, a liar! I was just going to lie to you then. To deceive you again. Now too, when I had made up my mind to tell you all.'

Jean's eyes spoke dumbly in her pale face. 'Go on,' they said.

Her lips were speechless.

'I let him think I wrote the book. Just at first, for a minute, I lost my head, but afterwards I could have convinced him if I had tried. I did not try. I let him think. I let him know.'

'He - thinks - you - wrote - it.' Her breath cut pauses between each word.

'I did write it.'

'What -tell me- what do you mean? What are you saying?'

'You think you wrote it. You believe that it has been a success because of what your pen put onto paper. But-(oh how can I tell her?)-but if I had not written in what I did write in, and left out what I did leave out, and altered everything, and thrown my whole soul into building up some substance out of your poor little trashy manuscript, the book would have been burnt by now, Jean, or making waste paper in some publisher's rubbish basket. No reader would have gone through fifty pages of it. It was my work that made the book. I wouldn't let you see that it was so. You never dreamt of it. You thought it was your work, and that my little alterations had had very little to do with the matter, but they made all the difference.'

He paused for breath.

'Do you remember the day you came to Monty's chambers?'

'Yes.' A little thin voice spoke.

'Well, I saw you coming. I knew you were at the door. I raised my voice purposely and praised your work, and called you a genius so that you would hear.'

He walked to the mantelpiece, and placed a fallen Chinese idol carefully on its feet. Then went on.

'I did not mean it. I believed-I believe still-that your talents as a literary woman are feminine in the extreme, and of the very smallest account. Jean, don't look at me! I called you a genius out of some feeling of spite for what I considered then your bad treatment of me. I knew it would be bad for you to hear me call you that. I knew you thought something of my opinions, even though you would not like me, or believe me. And when you had gone, I said to Harrison in these very words, as he reminded me to-day, "She hasn't as much literary ability as that poker, and not as much originality."

Jean was sitting now in the armchair, with her hands clenched in her lap.

'I told him I knew you would never do any good work, but that you would never believe it. I told him why I called you a genius. I believe I told him you had made me love you, and then had laughed at me. I almost believed that myself. I remember Harrison saying to me that it was a low thing to do. I laughed at him. I suppose I knew. I did know it, as a matter of fact, but I did it, nevertheless. I can do low things. I can be what men call a cad. I am a cad at times. I try to excuse myself to myself by virtue of my brains. I tell myself that any man with as good an intellect as mine must be a cad at times. I have a hundred sides. You know many of them, but not all. The one I am showing you now is a revelation. And I tell myself that I can't help being as I am, good, bad, honourable, and lowest of the low, all combined.'

Jean sat like a little frozen statue. Her face was death-like, grey. All the softness and childishness had gone out of it. The mouth was drawn into a queer little hard unnatural shape. Her eyes stared straight before her. Her hands were clenched so tightly that, for days after, the marks were red where the nails had made havoc of her fair soft flesh.

She did not say one word. Yet Musgrave, stealing a miserable look at her, read in her face a long succession of years wherein she would feel the smart and soreness of this night's story, and its bitterness.

His voice came from him, as from a man talking in his sleep.

He would go on; he would tell her all. It was as cruel a thing to add more grief to that little white hard face as to drive a nail into a dying man's heart, but this blessed numbness that was floating round his soul would help him through to the bitter end.

'That is not all,' he said. He waited. She still stared straight in front of her, and was silent. He went on.

'Elsa Macqueen-the girl who told you I had made love to her while I was doing my best to make you care for me-you believed her then. I told you it was a lie. You laughed at me. I determined that I would make you care for me, and believe me. You see I did both. I explained it all away to you afterwards, when you would listen to me. I told you how it might have happened - "Oh, nobody cares for me," and I had made some answer such as, "Don't say that. You know I like you, or perhaps, I care about you." You accepted that interpretation, and convinced yourself that she had misunderstood me. She did not misunderstand me. I did make love to her. God knows why; I don't, I did not care two straws for her. I loved you, but I made love to her all the same. I did not count upon her telling you.'

'It was true.'

She had spoken at last.

'Yes.'

'Ah-h-h-h.'

He had known that this would be the bitterest of all to her, but that little moaning 'ah,' almost theatrical in its intensity, told of a bitterness that made his heart sick to think of.

'Oh,' she said, 'is this all true?' She closed her eyes for a minute in a bewildered way, and put her hands to her forehead.

'It is true. I lied to you. I did not realise the truth and sweetness of your character at first, I loved you, but more for your brightness and your beauty than for the depths of womanliness you have revealed to me since. I deceived *you* all along. You cannot grasp it all at once. You will understand better afterwards.'

She was huddled up in a corner of her chair, and her head fell low on her arms, as they lay on the arm of the chair.

It seemed to Musgrave that a lifetime opened and closed before she spoke to him.

'Tell me this,' she said. 'Tell me one thing. Did you ever love me?'

When Musgrave looked at her she understood why he did not speak just at once. He could not.

Her breath was shortened suddenly. Those eyes of his with the tears in them! She was on her feet. She stood a moment where she was, then went towards him slowly, and passed behind his chair. She did not know what brought her there.

'I am glad-you-loved me,' she said. He buried his face in his arms, and she stood looking at him. The dark irregular waves of his hair gave her a pitiful feeling. It was such boyish hair, brown, and so curly. She put her hand out a little to touch it; then drew it back. What was he, this man here! What creature was he that he could bear himself so nobly, and look out on the world with such fine straight eyes, and act so degradingly, so meanly. He was the man she had loved. The man who had deceived her, lied to her, made sport of her; the man to whom she had laid bare, with childlike tenderness all the secret dreams and wanderings of her soul; the man who had kept his own soul hidden from her always, and shown her nothing of the man he really was.

'I don't realise it,' she kept saying to herself. 'I can't realise it.'

She tried to think what it all meant. Did it mean that she, who had tried so hard, and believed so in herself, was a desperate, miserable failure; a laughable, absurd pretension; a silly little butt for the world's and her friends' jests?

She remembered with an intolerable agony of mortification, the friend's words to her that afternoon in the study. 'You've no originality. You've no freshness. You've no wit. You've a certain amount of style, but it's borrowed. It's not characteristic. It is reminiscent. I hate your stories, and you can't write, Jean - you can't write.'

And she remembered what she had answered. 'Everyone does not think with you.'

It was of Musgrave she had been thinking when she had said that. Musgrave, who had praised and flattered and encouraged her; who had filled her with fresh hope day after day; upon whose opinion she had fattened and grown happy with self-confidence. Musgrave, whose judgment had been her one supreme reliance in her times of depression. Musgrave who had just now said to her with his own lips, 'I believe your talents as a literary woman to be feminine in the extreme, and of the very smallest account,' and who had summed her up long months ago as having as much literary ability as the poker, and not as much originality.

Strangely enough it never occurred to her to doubt the justness of the last verdict he had passed upon her work. She saw with an unerring eye that the end had come to all her vague conceits, her girlish hopes of a brilliant future, a great name, a little money, and a vast and comfortable assurance of herself. These were all over now. The fiat had gone forth. The man who had helped so tenderly and tirelessly to nurture them, had given them their death-blow.

And the book!

'I will not cry,' she was saying to herself. 'I will not lower myself to cry.'

Her brain, working round with the flashing convolutions that a supreme moment often arouses, began to think all manner of strange and irrelevant thoughts.

She wondered if she had sewn that button firmly enough on the waistband of Star's white dress. If the skirt came off while they were playing Musical Chairs, and it caught in some child's foot, and was kicked away across the room, and somebody else tripped over it, and kicked it on into somebody else's way. As the music quickened, they would toss it on and on round the room, laughing and shrieking as they rushed along. Her brain was filled with the giddy image of a white skirt being whisked and whirled through the air and round the room, over the children's heads, under their stamping feet. Round and round, under and over. Her eyes were strained with trying to follow all the eccentricities of that white thing's flight, and her brain reeled a little. Her hands were trembling. Musgrave waited for her to go. He told himself that all was over now. He sat by the table with his head bowed down upon his arms, and his mind wandering dully from one miserable thought to another. He waited a long time.

Upstairs the strains of light child voices told of the revelry of Star's birthday-party. Little shrill laughs, and clear high calls, and speeches came floating down the stairway to these two who were alone here.

The careless, happy sweetness of the little children's voices, smote through this silence and deepened it. It became a sadder thing even than before.

It was Jean who broke it. She rose, and moved across the room, and Musgrave heard the door close gently behind her. He did not raise his head. He was saying to himself that there should be at least one evil thing he would not do; he would not try, by word or look, to hold her to him. When the door closed on her, and he believed that she had left him, an actual physical faintness came upon him, and for two or three minutes he lost all consciousness of himself.

Presently he heard the door pushed open again. Someone came in. He heard Jean's footsteps on the floor behind him.

She had come back. She was moving about the room. Then he heard the rustling of loose paper. She seemed to be carrying things across the room towards the fireplace.

At last she stopped. She was standing by his chair. 'Will you give me a match?' she said.

There on the hearthstone was a pile of manuscript that reached even past the level of the grate's top rung. It was the work of a girl's life-time. There were exercise books with stories begun long years before, and never finished; copies of a school magazine in manuscript, for which Jean had written when her hair hung in a pig-tail down her back; the first rough drafts of her book - that had never been hers - the scribbled originals of many a tale and article; and the only copy of the book that was not yet finished.

She had piled them altogether there.

'I want you to give me the match,' she said again.

'I - cannot.'

'You owe me that much.'

She held her hand out to him and waited. He turned away, and walked to the other end of the room.

There was a candle burning on the table. She caught it up, and, going down on her knees, held it against the ink-covered papers, and watched them as the blue flame licked them over and over into its embrace.

'Let them burn,' she said. 'I give it up for ever.'

Perhaps in her heart of hearts as the flame rolled over them, a wish may have arisen that Musgrave would interfere even now, and try to rescue them.

But he made no move. He knew their worthlessness.

'What a farce it has been,' he heard Jean saying, half to herself. 'There, let them burn. This is the end of it all. Serve me right, little silly *fool.'*

She caught her breath.

'It is better for them to burn, isn't it?' she said. She was not looking at him, but she waited for his answer. 'Isn't it best that they should burn?'

And, 'Yes. It is the best thing,' he replied. He was telling himself that women were cruel beings. He could never have tortured Jean as she was torturing him.

'It is such a simple thing too,' she said, ' just a match, and a little blaze, and the whole sickening story comes to an end. And you have never had the courage to light the match. You have let me go on, and on; you have seen the nature of the dead sea apples I have strained my soul to gather. No, no, I don't want to be hard. I don't want to be cruel, but how *could* you do it, how *could* you, how *could* you. Oh, how miserable I am. You never loved me. You could never have loved me. Oh, come here. Come close to me. Let me look at you. Let me see into your eyes.'

But Musgrave could not turn to her, and she stood by the smouldering ashes of her dreams, alone.

'It does me good to look at those ashes. I know now that all those things are out of my reach. When I went out of the room just now I went to my own room and threw myself on the bed, and told myself how I loathed you, how I despised you. I am no grand woman. What I minded most was that you could have let me deceive myself about my work. Oh, *nobody* knows how I love it! Can it be possible to love it as I do, and have no fitness for it? ... Surely ... '

But he was utterly silent.

'Look at me. You must. Look straight into my eyes. Are you right? Are you sure you are right? And do other men think so too? If I go on trying, working hard?'

He still kept silence.

'And my friend? Will she ever make a name?'

'I think so,' said Musgrave.

'And you know,' Jean said hopelessly. Then she too kept silence.

'There is only one thing now for me to do,' said Musgrave.

'To go away. I ought to have done it before.'

'Where are you going? Wait. *Was it hard to tell me?*'

'Jean .. .'

'Was it hard? Was it terribly, excruciatingly hard? *I* could never have done it.'

'For God's sake don't make any excuses for me. I could never have confessed. I would have gone away; I would never have told you. I *couldn't.*'

He had turned away, and was sitting again with his head bowed down in his hand.

Suddenly Jean came behind him, and a rain of quick passionate kisses fell on his hair; they startled him, they were not like Jean's kisses.

'Oh, I love you, I love you, I love you. Do you think I could let you go? No, no. I love you. God decided that long ago for me. It is not in my hands. I have not changed to you. I cannot change. I love you for yourself, for your eyes, and voice, and hair, and strength, for everything that belongs to you, and for this last thing, this wrong to me, *more than all.'*

She went on kissing his hair, with her arms round his neck, and his head so close against her heart that the little paste buttons of her gown were cutting into his cheek.

'Oh, my God! Her forgiveness hurts more than any punishment.'

His voice was low, but she heard him.

'Dearest, I *love* you.' Her warm breath was in his ear. 'There is no forgiveness. Only love.'

She was murmuring something over his head. He caught the echo of three words.

'Christ,' and 'Help,' and 'Bless.'

He turned, and held her in his arms. Her eyelids fell over her eyes; the sweetness of her mouth was indescribable. A sort of rapture was on her upturned face. It reminded Musgrave, even at that moment, of Rossetti's wonderful 'Beata Beatrix,' picture.

'Oh, my Saint, my Saint! Oh, you noble woman! You are a grander woman than you ever dreamed of being. Oh, Jean, Jean, is it possible? Little Jean, can you love me still?'

'Kiss me, kiss me.'

'You were a little girl before,' he said afterwards.' You are a woman now. The difference is in your kisses.'

'Let us begin all over again. You told me, and with the telling it is all wiped out. We will begin all over again.'

Musgrave knew then that his punishment was to come from himself. He knew that, for himself, there could be no such thing as an absolute wiping out. As long as he loved Jean he would remember.

'I have been wicked too,' said Jean. 'I have been horrid. You don't know. I let Mr Harrison put his hand on my head one night, and keep it there a minute. I think he stroked my hair. It was my fault. I wasn't angry with him. I-I-perhaps I liked it. I knew he liked me, and I wanted him to, and I belonged to you. I want everyone to like me. Sometimes I try to make them. I feel that they must like me, and I make them. I don't know whether I ever tried to make Mr Harrison.

Yes, yes. I did - I think.'

'He loved you,' said Musgrave in a low voice. Neither of them noticed that they used the past tense.

'No, no,' said Jean. She hid her face in her hands.

'I know it,' said Musgrave. 'I have always known it.'

'He was lonely,' said Jean. 'He liked me. He thought me pretty. He-he-was fond of me and of Star too. He knew hardly any other girls. He thought he liked me, but he never really cared for me.'

The Post Office clock was striking ten o'clock across the city, and Harrison, away in his lonely attic, was watching his star for the last time. Already it was fading from his sight. His eyes were darkening on this little world below, perhaps to see no other, perhaps to open on a wider. And 'Jean' was on his dying lips.

'Not as I care,' said Musgrave, huskily, 'nobody could.' She believed him, for she loved him, and she had never loved Harrison.

Printed in Australia
AUHW020833060821
349953AU00002B/7